Praise for *I'll Just Be Five*

"These essays feel like catching up with an old friend that I actually like listening to. If you enjoy my flavor of OCD you will have just as much fun at Emily's ADHD party."

—Samantha Irby, *New York Times* best-selling author of *Quietly Hostile* and self-described idiot jokester

"Funny, cringey, and oh-so relatable."

—Jenny Lawson, *New York Times* best-selling author of *Broken* and *Furiously Happy*

"Not only is this memoir witty, laugh-out-loud funny, enlightening, and brave, it also perfectly fits a reader who has ADHD. Short chapters, pithy sentences, fresh insights, *nothing boring*. Aimed at the largest undiagnosed group—adult women with ADHD— Farris tells her story in such an engagingly personal way that it appeals to everyone. It instructs by pleasing. Bravo, Emily Farris!"

—Edward Hallowell, M.D., author most recently of *ADHD 2.0*

"I picked up *I'll Just Be Five More Minutes* intending to peek at the first few lines. Four hours later, I was still on the couch, intermittently laughing and nodding my head in recognition. This is an ignore-your-family, cancel-your-plans, stay-up-past-your-bedtime tale that reminds me of Samantha Irby, David Sedaris, and so many other favorite essayists. It's laugh-out-loud funny and strikingly smart, and Farris offers brilliant insight into the ADHD brain."

—Joanna Rakoff, best-selling author of *My Salinger Year*

"Emily Farris has written a book that will stay with me forever: hilarious, insightful, and with a voice reminiscent of Davids Rakoff and Sedaris, Farris takes on what it means to have a neurodivergent brain in a neurotypical world, and how her discovery at age thirty-five that she had ADHD resulted in the pieces of her life suddenly clicking into place like the glass in a kaleidoscope. Completely relatable, wise, warm, and very funny. I loved it." —Elissa Altman, author of *Motherland*

"I am a lifelong flailer and noted scatterbrain, and Emily Farris's warm, wise, and very funny book not only makes me feel seen but makes me wonder if maybe I shouldn't have sought help long ago. No matter how your brain works, this book will make you want to be her best friend."
—Emily Flake, Cartoonist for *The New Yorker*

"Emily Farris's debut hits all the big topics: life, love, and, yes, even lipstick. Yet these eminently readable essays go down smoother than the sweet pink wine cooler that young Emily might have thrown back before embarking on an ill-fated but hilarious adventure. *I'll Just Be Five More Minutes* is an unputdownable book that offers a frank, funny look at the highs and lows of life with a neurodivergent brain."
—Amy Shearn, award-winning author of *Unseen City,*
The Mermaid of Brooklyn, and other novels

I'll Just Be Five More Minutes

I'll Just Be Five More Minutes

(And Other Tales from My ADHD Brain)

Emily Farris

hachette
BOOKS
NEW YORK

Hachette Books
Hachette Book Group
1290 Avenue of the Americas
New York, NY 10104
HachetteBooks.com
Twitter.com/HachetteBooks
Instagram.com/HachetteBooks

First Edition: February 2024

Published by Hachette Books, an imprint of Perseus Books, LLC,
a subsidiary of Hachette Book Group, Inc. The Hachette Books
name and logo are trademarks of the Hachette Book Group.

The Hachette Speakers Bureau provides a wide range of authors for
speaking events. To find out more, go to hachettespeakersbureau.com or
email HachetteSpeakers@hbgusa.com.

Books by Hachette Books may be purchased in bulk for business, educational, or
promotional use. For information, please contact your local bookseller or Hachette
Book Group Special Markets Department at: Special.Markets@hbgusa.com.

The publisher is not responsible for websites (or their content)
that are not owned by the publisher.

Print book interior design by Bart Dawson.

Library of Congress Cataloging-in-Publication Data
Name: Farris, Emily, author.
Title: I'll just be five more minutes: and other tales from my
ADHD brain / Emily Farris.
Description: First edition. | New York: Hachette Books, 2024. |
Includes bibliographical references.
Identifiers: LCCN 2023018885 | ISBN 9780306830310 (trade paperback) |
ISBN 9780306830327 (ebook)
Subjects: LCSH: Farris, Emily. | Farris, Emily—Mental health. |
Attention-deficit-disordered adults—United States—Biography. |
Attention-deficit-disordered women—United States—Biography. |
Attention-deficit disorder in adults—Popular works.
Classification: LCC RC394.A85 F37 2024 | DDC
616.85/890092—dc23/eng/20230925
LC record available at https://lccn.loc.gov/2023018885

ISBNs: 9780306830310 (trade paperback); 9780306830327 (ebook)

Printed in the United States of America

LSC-C

Printing 3, 2024

My own brain is to me the most unaccountable of machinery—always buzzing, humming, soaring roaring diving, and then buried in mud. And why? What's this passion for?

—Virginia Woolf

Contents

A Very Not-Chronological Retelling
of My Life So Far

Author's Note

Save for the obvious satire, everything in this book actually happened and is written to the best of my recollection.

I turned to old emails, blog posts, and news reports to corroborate my memories whenever possible and checked in with my little sister a lot, too. Sadly, I could not recall my MySpace password—but maybe that's for the best. Though some dialogue is paraphrased, it is all true to the spirit and tone of the conversations that took place. Additionally, a few timelines were condensed to spare you boring details and I've changed the names and identifying characteristics of certain people in an attempt to preserve their anonymity (including the ones who don't deserve it).

Introduction

Part I: Words About My Life

I should have been proud of myself. It was September 2018, and my family's first holiday card was almost ready to be mailed. Half were even addressed. The only problem? They were 2017's cards. And because I didn't get them done until after Christmas, they said "Happy New Year!" instead of "Happy Holidays!"

Still, I had every intention of sending the expired greetings—though mostly as a joke. Because, really, what the hell else was I supposed to do with them? Plus, the photo of my little family was super cute; I'd spent a week coordinating our outfits and we paid a professional photographer to make sure the light wouldn't accentuate any of our extra chins. Anyone who knows me would have been shocked and delighted to get any kind of mail from me, though not at all surprised when they noticed that my then three-year-old son, Teddy, was pretty much still a baby in the picture.

For years those cards sat in a drawer—I call it my Drawer of Doom—until the day I impulsively swapped out the Art Deco buffet we'd been using as a bar for a wall-mounted unit.

When I cleaned out the old bar, I was forced to confront other things I'd shoved in that drawer along with the cards: graduation announcements I'd convinced myself I'd someday send gifts for, a thick stack of certified mail from the IRS I was afraid to open, overdue medical bills I had opened but hadn't paid, and at least sixty dollars' worth of winning but very expired scratch-off lottery tickets. The lottery tickets were trash (which I know because once, when I was really broke, I had tried to cash in old scratch-offs), but the rest went into a plastic bin I shoved into a closet because, though I was medicated by that point, it was all too overwhelming.

My paperwork problem is technically an "executive dysfunction," a term used by mental health practitioners to describe difficulties with cognitive, organizational, and emotional tasks. But until I was diagnosed with attention deficit hyperactivity disorder (ADHD) at age thirty-five, I—and nearly everyone I knew along with lots of people in offices I didn't know—saw my paperwork problem as a "character flaw." Sure, I was a published writer with a family, a gaggle of internet fans, and (most shockingly) a mortgage, but I could never get my shit together. At least not for more than a few weeks at a time, anyway.

In hindsight, my combined type ADHD makes so much sense. I was a kid with a quick temper and a serious lack of impulse control. I interrupted sentences (my own included) with new ideas (brilliant ones, of course!), and I'd often get late-night bursts of inspiration that kept me up doing crafty projects way past my bedtime. My brain was always on overdrive, and I hated how slowly the rest of my little world moved in comparison, even in elementary school.

One of my earliest academic disappointments happened when I was six. I wrote a letter to my first-grade teacher on lined notebook paper, asking if we could skip ahead in our math textbook because I was bored with addition and subtraction. She wrote me back, which was very sweet, but her reply instructed me to be patient, so I decided I hated math. Now, as a forty-year-old writer, I can barely do basic arithmetic without a calculator.

And you know what? I'm too busy working seventeen jobs and actively avoiding the mountains of dirty laundry in my basement to be retroactively mad at one elementary school teacher—or every adult I ever knew—for missing the signs. Still, every once in a while, I wonder what would have happened if I had been academically challenged in the ways I was begging to be.

Instead of using what my friend Ann calls "the magic brain" to make great art or, like, win a math-a-thon (is that a real thing? I'm too lazy to look it up even though I'm currently typing on a computer that's connected to the internet), my mental energy was reserved for cleaning up my own messes. (Exhibit A: Talking my way out of detention after I'd been sent to the principal's office for talking too much in class—which worked 99 percent of the time, by the way.)

To make matters worse, things weren't great at home. My parents divorced when I was three and my mom was dealing with her own problems, so she took care of what she could see and feel, like rashes and fevers, but there wasn't anything left for the less tangible issues. I craved attention except when I wanted solitude, and I didn't really get either—in part because, as I got older, I felt the burden of my much more timid younger sister Jo's well-being. Sometimes I joke to Jo now that I was thrown into the role of teen mom when I was only four and she was three—a real babies-raising-babies situation.

Maybe it's that I understood no one was overly concerned with my needs, but I became a very angry—and self-conscious—kid. At a young age, I began to hyperfocus on the way adults interacted with me. I read their facial expressions and body language and fixated on the tone of their voices. It didn't take long to figure out that when someone said I was "precocious," they really meant "obnoxious."

At school, I put on a happy face. Probably because that's where I got the most validation. It wasn't from other students—until I had my first sip of a pink wine cooler, I struggled socially—but from the handful of teachers who were delighted by my lust for learning their chosen subject matter. My early enthusiasm for task-based work meant I was the kid who did the group project by myself because everyone else would just slow me down and there was no way in hell I was going to let Ashlee, Ashley, Ashleigh, and Brandon fuck up my amazing diorama. I got straight As without trying, did extra-credit assignments just for fun, and stimulated my brain by overloading my schedule with a rotating lineup of extracurricular activities. When I got bored with one thing (or unduly frustrated by my peers' less-than-enthusiastic participation), I'd move on to the next, seemingly wasting what educators claimed was my "great potential."

By the time I graduated high school, I had somehow earned a reputation as both an overachiever *and* an underachiever, which sounds impossible, but I promise you, it's not.

Later, my sporadic attempts to be more like people who had savings accounts and organized closets included going to bed before midnight exactly once and putting away clean laundry a couple times a year. Occasionally, I'd read the first few chapters of the latest self-help book about productivity or financial freedom and get really serious about being A Responsible Adult. But none of it ever stuck and I finally accepted that I was just kind of a mess, maybe even a lazy asshole. At some point, it became part of my identity.

After my diagnosis, my husband, Kyle, admitted that a few months into marriage he felt like I'd pulled a switcheroo because I stopped focusing on him. What neither of us knew at the time was that I was having a typical ADHD reaction to the end of a big event—actually, a series of big events: Over the course of fewer than three years, I met a man I really liked, went on lots of fun dates, and fell in love. Then he moved into my apartment, we traveled some, moved into a new house together, and got engaged. The climax was an amazing barn party with an open bar, two live bands, and a sweet little ceremony at the start. But after the excitement of our wedding weekend, my brain was having what one study called "a dysfunction in the brain reward cascade" (aka a big, stinky brain fart).

My life is peppered with those dysfunctional moments. If I were a boy (and perhaps had grown up in a more affluent corner of the world), a teacher or school counselor might have suggested I get screened for ADHD instead of telling me to try harder and lecturing me about my tardiness and lack of follow-through. But like so many neurodivergent women and girls (and people of color and, really, anyone but cis white men), I internalized the criticisms and carried around a lot of shame while I exhausted myself trying to fit into a world that was not built for my brain.

And those are the stories I tell in this book.

It's estimated that ten million adults in the United States have ADHD. While I imagine most of my readers are neurodivergent themselves (also the people who know and love them), I'd like to think many of my experiences are more universally relatable. At their heart, these are stories about not quite fitting in to the world and, for most of my life, not really understanding why—something even neurotypical folks have felt at one time or another. Plus, there's all kinds of fun stuff in here: sex, drama, a dead body, and most tantalizing, a celebrity stalker (which, I admit, is not the most relatable thing I've ever written).

Part II: Words About Words

I know we're all very excited to get to the drama and the drugs and the thing about the celebrity who threatened to destroy my life, but before we do, a little housekeeping.

The Doctor Is Not In

I am not a mental health professional nor an expert on neuroscience, and the only story I can tell is my own. That means you won't find any self-help or diagnostic tools in this book. There's no advice either. But if you have ADHD and you want to feel seen, or you're trying to better understand someone with ADHD (or you're just trying to get through this for book club), you've come to the right place. That said, I can't very well write sixty thousand words about my not-so-normal brain without first explaining some of the terms and concepts used herein. So, just so we're all on the same page, here's a little primer on ADHD followed by an answer to what I know is your most burning question.

What Is ADHD?

Attention deficit hyperactivity disorder (ADHD) is a neurodevelopmental "disorder" that's usually diagnosed in childhood—unless, of course, it's missed. Although the exact cause of ADHD is still unknown, studies point to genetic factors combined with certain environmental risks (and watching too much TV is not one of them). But there's still plenty we do know.

Studying the brains of people with ADHD has shown a dysfunction in the dopaminergic system, meaning ADHD brains don't process dopamine the way "normal" (neurotypical) brains do. Dopamine controls numerous brain functions, including attention, mood, cognition, reward, and movement, which helps explain why neurodivergent people may struggle in those areas.

Despite what naysayers would like you to believe, ADHD is not some trendy new diagnosis made up to sell prescription drugs. Though it didn't yet have a name, the first textbook description of a condition that presented as ADHD appeared in 1775, and the first recorded description of ADHD was published in 1902 under the title "Some Abnormal Psychical Conditions in Children."

Neurodiverse versus Neurodivergent

My brain is a poetic, noble land-mermaid brain. It's also neurodivergent. This is not to be confused with the term "neurodiverse," which encompasses *all* the different ways brains experience the world—including neurotypical *and* neurodivergent brains. Our interpretation of language is always evolving, but as I write this in 2023, "neurodiverse" is still used incorrectly as a blanket term for people with clinical neurological differences like ADHD, autism, dyspraxia, and dyslexia. But if you want to use a blanket term for those of us who are not neurotypical, the proper one is "neurodivergent" (though in recent years, some of my favorite online spaces have embraced "neurospicy," which I also love).

I Write About ADHD Symptoms, but I Usually Don't Point Them Out

Have I mentioned I'm not a mental health professional? Okay, now that we have that out of the way yet again, I want to briefly go over some of the symptoms that appear in this book because I don't really get into them in my essays. But please keep in mind this is by no means an exhaustive list of ADHD symptoms; these are simple explanations shared through the lens of my own experiences.

EXECUTIVE DYSFUNCTION

"Executive dysfunction" is kind of a blanket term used to describe difficulties with cognitive, organizational, and emotional tasks—basically, all the brain functions that help people get shit done and maintain healthy relationships.

HYPERFIXATION

At work or school, people with ADHD may be more easily distracted than their neurotypical peers, but good luck trying to divert our focus from our interest du jour. Once we become hyperfixated or hyperfocused on a particular project or task, it consumes our attention—often at the expense of everything else in our lives, including eating, sleeping, showering, and sometimes even getting up to pee. This can be a real problem for those of us with kids, spouses, and jobs, but it's also kind of a superpower because many of us use it to teach ourselves new skills literally overnight. Which brings us to . . .

TIME BLINDNESS

The term "time blindness" refers to an inability to properly perceive the passing of time. People with ADHD often underestimate how long it will take to get something done and can become so focused on a particular task—or distracted by a subtask or possibly a completely unrelated one—that we have no real sense of how long we've been at it. This explains why people with ADHD may be late for everything, or sometimes seem unreasonably busy but have little to show for it—and it inspired the title of this book!

EMOTIONAL REGULATION

People with ADHD often have extreme emotional reactions to criticism or disapproval, which can show up in the form of angry outbursts, sadness, and anxiety, as well as people-pleasing and perfectionist tendencies. If you've spent any time on #ADHDTikTok, you've surely seen references to RSD, or rejection-sensitive dysphoria, which is described as a disproportionate or severe emotional response to real or perceived criticism or rejection. There's some debate in the mental health community around the existence of RSD, and as I finish this book in 2023, it's not formally recognized as a disorder. Since I'm not a medical professional (have I mentioned that yet?), I can only speak from my personal experience, which is that my undiagnosed ADHD caused a lot of unnecessary trauma that worsened my symptoms. I've also had to work really hard to hide my messy parts, so of course I'm going to have seemingly overblown reactions to anything that feels like rejection—especially when it comes from the people closest to me.

SENSORY PROCESSING ISSUES

Though sensory processing issues are more commonly associated with autism (which sometimes occurs with ADHD), some people with ADHD also experience hypersensitivity to certain sound, touch, or smell stimuli. For me, this manifests as a severe aversion to all fruit in its solid form. I'm easily overstimulated by noise and want to run away when my husband and kids talk to me at the same damn time. Also, I can't rub my hands on any fabric, ever, and I can't even put a finger on a towel or touch my shirt while I'm brushing my teeth (weirdly specific, I know).

The mere experience of watching someone rub their hand on their jeans will send me running into the other room. It's so bad I got the heebie-jeebies writing those words!

——————————

Other recurring themes include intensity, impulsivity, over-thinking, social anxiety, postpartum anxiety, pandemic anxiety, and substance abuse—because people with undiagnosed ADHD sometimes try to self-medicate without realizing it (I get into this a little in my essay "Street Drugs"). Some of the symptoms overlap, some feed each other, blah, blah, blah, I'm a writer, not a doctor.

How I Wrote This Book

If you've made it this far, you're probably wondering, "Emily, how the hell did you, a person with ADHD, write a whole-ass book over the course of a single year, while also holding a full-time staff writing job and being a wife and a mom to two small kids?!" And that is a very good question (except you forgot to include the weekly podcast, though I had to put that on indefinite hiatus a few months in because I didn't want to die).

First of all, none of this would be possible without Vyvanse (the brand name for my prescribed stimulant medication). But even with meds, I had to implement a slew of systems to make it work, including rolling deadlines and monthly check-ins with my editor, plus back-to-back writing workshops to keep me motivated and accountable. I also went further into debt than I already was (more on that later) to put a little writing studio in my backyard so I'd be less tempted to rearrange the furniture in my house seventy-five times instead of putting words on the page. I call it The Fancy Shed, because it is a shed that is fancy.

Still, completing an entire manuscript was rough, mostly because I never felt like I had enough time to write. When I did find little windows, it was rarely more than an hour or two. If it was after I'd put my kids to bed (which it usually was) and my meds had worn off, and I wasn't excited about what I was writing, I couldn't make anything coherent come out. Other times I was just too tired. Or I'd start to write and one of my sons would wake up vomiting. Or we all got Covid and I didn't touch the manuscript for a month. Or Kyle and I would get into a fight and I'd be too emotionally exhausted to psycho-analyze my brain, so I'd eat Doritos and binge-watch medical dramas. Sometimes I just thought *fuck it* and made some jokes or poked fun at myself and that's a hundred percent how I deal with stress and discomfort in real life, too.

I'm pretty sure I disappointed many people over the last year, I don't think I exercised once, and I know for certain I didn't shower often enough. And because I started a full-time commerce writing job at Epicurious right around the time I signed on to do the book, I have no clue what it's like to work one job without also doing this other huge thing. So everybody please leave me alone for a while. (Kidding, of course. You can call me any time, Terry Gross!)

It wasn't all bad, though, and not only because I got to spend a lot of time alone in The Fancy Shed. I realize what an incredible privilege it is to be given a chance to tell my story in book form and that I had the resources to get it done. Some-times reminding myself of that would send me into one of those headspaces writers dream of, when I knew exactly what I wanted to write and the perfect words poured out of me on the first try. Those are some of my favorite essays in the book, but I'll let you guess which ones they are.

Speaking of privilege, it also helps to have a really great sup-port system. A Nespresso machine, too. And if it makes you feel any better, as I write this sentence, I'm about sixteen hours from my deadline, so even with my stimulants and accountabil-ity tools and The Fancy Shed, I'm still flying by the seat of my pants!

How to Read This Book

Like my brain, the essays I share on these pages are all over the place. Because the events aren't always presented in chronolog-ical order—or even in a traditional essay format—you might be tempted to skip around, but I advise against it since some people are introduced in detail in earlier essays and later just mentioned by their first names. Plus, callbacks to my methy hometown make more sense after you've read the essay about my methy hometown.

Neurodivergent readers may prefer to read from a hard copy and listen at the same time (or just listen), so I'd like to point out that this title is also available as an audiobook, nar-rated by yours truly. And obviously, I want you to buy as many copies in as many formats as your little heart desires because the more you buy, the closer I am to getting my financial shit together. So with that in mind, you might as well buy one for a friend while you're at it!

_____

Okay, now you're ready to proceed to the juicy bits. I hope you enjoy reading it ~~as much as~~ more than I enjoyed writing it. And if you don't, just know that I'll obsess over your terrible review for the rest of my life.

I'll Just Be Five More Minutes

How We Got Here
The Diagnosis That Saved My Marriage

On our first anniversary, after a few too many Old Fash-
ioneds, I asked my husband if he regretted marrying me.
"I wouldn't exactly call it regret," he said.

He spent the next twenty minutes trying to explain his
answer, but I didn't hear any of it. I was certain this signaled the
end of my marriage, so I gave up mixing cocktails and started
panic-drinking whiskey, then cried myself to sleep. The next
morning, with clearer (but throbbing) heads, he apologized and
I promised to try harder.

Kyle had been eager to settle into the routine of married
life. I thought I wanted that, too, but early on we both started
to sense that I was more suited to the spontaneity and autonomy Dating Seriously allowed.

We met in our late twenties after we'd both made our way
back to Kansas City—me from a decade in Brooklyn and him
from eighteen months teaching English in Korea. By the end of
our first date, we'd planned our next three and I quickly learned

he showed his love by cooking elaborate meals and burning mix CDs well beyond the time that was a thing. Two years later, we exchanged vows at a very-2012 barn party.

But not long after we said "I do," I began to panic about the fact that I'd just committed the rest of my life to someone who wanted to know my plan: for the evening, for the weekend, for his next trip to Costco. That's a reasonable expectation in most relationships, but the problem—as my new groom saw it, anyway—was that there weren't any plans. For as long as I can remember, I ate when I was so hungry it hurt and stumbled into bed when I could no longer keep my eyes open. The only thing I'd ever bought in bulk was my favorite red lipstick once I learned it was being discontinued.

Before Kyle, my life had mostly been a series of false starts—the perfect job, the perfect apartment, the perfect guy. Eventually, they all began to feel like an itchy sweater I was desperate to take off, so I'd make some sweeping change and start over. Kyle was more like a favorite sweatshirt that got a little too tight after marriage. He'd ask questions I couldn't answer, like: "How can you spend three hours arguing with Republicans on Facebook, but you won't hang out with your husband for fifteen minutes?" and "Why don't you ever come to bed with me?" I pulled a blanket over my head when he tried to talk about money and pulled away when he wanted to talk about our relationship.

Nothing he was asking for was objectively unattainable; I just couldn't quite seem to attain it. And every few weeks he'd send me some article that boiled down to what I'd heard from teachers, self-help audiobooks, and bosses my whole life: you're not trying hard enough.

I didn't want to lose him (and not just because he made sure I ate at least one real meal a day), so I skimmed most of the articles he sent, doubled my caffeine intake, and became overly dependent on calendar reminders. I made a budget spreadsheet I compulsively updated for about a month and set notifications for everything, including "Check In with Kyle" on weekdays to discuss our plans (or lack thereof) for the evening. And most days I did check in. Until I stopped.

After our worst fights, I'd cry in the shower, wondering how many more times I could mess up before he'd divorce me. Because no matter how hard I tried, I somehow always found a way to self-destruct.

When I got pregnant a few years later, I decided something had to change. This kid wasn't choosing to have me as a mother, so I turned all my attention to preparing for the baby. I joined Facebook groups with people who worried way too much about soft cheese and stretch marks, and I amassed piles of parenting books I believed I'd someday read.

Save for a rough start to breastfeeding and some undiagnosed postpartum anxiety, the first year of motherhood was much smoother than the first year of marriage. Kyle and I were so in love with our son Teddy that we put our relationship problems on the back burner. I became militant about baby sleep schedules and mealtimes and even kept up with washing and putting away miniature clothes for twelve whole months. I was shockingly content giving my full self to this tiny human who relied on me for everything and never demanded to have a serious talk about money or asked if I'd given any thought to dinner.

Shortly after Teddy's first birthday, I accepted what seemed like the perfect job managing social media for a restaurant group. I was excited to leave the house in real clothes and use my brain for something other than playing peekaboo and reciting *Goodnight Moon* from memory. Incessant notifications and bad reviews demanded my immediate attention. It was thrilling.

At home, laundry piled up. Mornings were total chaos. Kyle and I started fighting again.

One evening, when things seemed to be going smoothly, he asked if I could maybe make dinner for us only once a month. "It can be something easy, like that roast chicken you used to make."

Oh! The roast chicken I used to make when I was a freelancer and didn't have a toddler who demanded my attention all the time? THAT fucking roast chicken?

I was too upset to say that, but I did start crying. Though really it was more of a wail.

"I don't understand how women have kids *and* jobs and ever cook or clean or do anything ever at all!"

We ordered takeout and he talked me down. But the sense of calm didn't last. If I was doing one thing right, I was doing everything else wrong. As hard as I tried, there was simply no way for me to be a good partner, a good mother, *and* a good employee.

On our fifth anniversary, Kyle (ever the optimist) surprised me with a reservation for a weekend away in a luxury treehouse. He wisely gave me two months' notice so I wouldn't have to stress over last-minute travel. I spent the weeks leading up to our trip focused on working ahead so I could leave my laptop at home and be fully present with my husband (as present as one can be from a heart-shaped jacuzzi overlooking the Ozark Mountains, anyway). I finally felt on top of my shit.

Apparently, I was a little too on top of my shit, though, because the weekend before we were supposed to leave, I showed up for a brunch a day early. I laughed it off and took it as a reminder to double-check the arrangements I'd made for our little getaway.

First, I texted the dog sitter: "Just confirming: I'll bring the dogs to you on Thursday."

Next, the babysitter: "Remember you have Friday off!"

Then my in-laws: "Finalizing details for next weekend. You're picking up Teddy from school Thursday and keeping him through Sunday, yes?"

Kyle's mom replied first: "But aren't you going out of town the weekend after next?"

Sweat started to seep out of the weird places it does when I get nervous (palms, underboob, and where my ass meets my thighs) and I scrambled to find the email confirmation for the treehouse. I exhaled when I saw I had the right departure date. Then I looked at my phone's lock screen and realized my real problem: I had no concept of that date in relation to the one I was living in. I didn't know *when* I was.

I went through the familiar motions of cleaning up my scheduling mess and everything was fine until that Friday. The babysitter was late, so I sent her a text: "Hi. Where are you?? Close, I hope!"

Her reply knocked the wind out of me: "In Wichita. And you're in a treehouse in Arkansas. Right?!"

I'd forgotten to reschedule the babysitter.

How was I still fucking up so badly?

In my quest for answers during the first year of supposed marital bliss, I'd happened upon an article called "ADHD Is Different for Women." So much of it had felt familiar: the sense of not being able to hold everything together, the disorganization, the forgetfulness, and especially the internalized shame. (See also: moldy coffee cups all over the damn place.) At the time, I convinced myself an ADHD diagnosis would be too easy. I just needed to go to bed earlier and open my mail and exercise and look at my calendar more often. And maybe throw in some turmeric tea and quit gluten. I needed to *try harder*.

Back then, I'd willed myself to dismiss the article, but it always lived somewhere in the back of my mind, and I was suddenly desperate to read it again. I texted my boss with one hand, put on *Daniel Tiger* for Teddy with the other, then furiously typed something about women and ADHD and moldy mugs into my phone's browser. Rereading it a few years later, I zeroed in on a big point I'd forgotten: women often mask their symptoms until their thirties when marriage and motherhood become so stressful that they hit a wall.

For the first time, I started to let myself believe there might be something clinically wrong with my brain. Maybe it wasn't a matter of not trying hard enough; maybe I wasn't getting enough dopamine to function like a neurotypical person. The thought came with a rush of sadness and relief. And lots of tears.

I sent Kyle a link to the article with one word: "Me."

He replied a few minutes later: "This is crazy, babe. It totally sounds like you."

Then: "You should see a doctor, too. If medication will make your quality of life markedly better, you deserve that."

I did deserve that. We both did. I deserved less stress and shame, and Kyle deserved a wife whose brain processed dopamine like the woman he thought he married.

As soon as we returned from our magical treehouse weekend, I attempted to find a doctor to guide me through treatment. It was harder than it should have been, though; my first couple of visits were with a psychiatry resident who tried to convince me I had bipolar disorder—for which I would have gladly accepted a diagnosis and treatment if I believed it were true. But at the risk of sounding like an anti-vaxxer, I'd done enough of my own research to know it wasn't the issue. My insurance company wasn't much help when I tried to find another provider, so I started asking around for someone who would, at the very least, believe the things I told them.

It took a few months, but I found a psychologist—we'll call her Dr. B—who specialized in ADHD and, shockingly, she was accepting new patients (which might have had something to do with her office being a thirty-five-minute drive outside of the city). So what that she didn't take my insurance? Or that she couldn't even prescribe meds? I was so desperate for someone to take me seriously that I was more than happy to give her all my money along with my abridged life story over the course of a few fifty-minute sessions.

Dr. B not only took me seriously but also validated my feelings—and the more I talked, the more I realized how many of my flaws were likely ADHD symptoms. And the more dots I connected, the more I cried. I cried because I was relieved to have an explanation and also because I was sad for how hard everyone (including me) had been on my younger self.

My final session with Dr. B was less emotionally fraught. It was surprisingly kinda fun. She performed a series of cognitive tests as part of a more official ADHD evaluation. I blew her mind with some of my abilities (like repeating a ridiculously long series of random numbers) and we both laughed when my short-term memory failed me miserably (like when I had to repeat anything in backward order and never got past the first word, character, or digit).

"I can't believe you made it to thirty-five without anyone figuring this out," Dr. B said as she handed me a referral sheet she'd filled out by hand.

"Almost thirty-six," I said, noticing that on the line for diagnosis, she had written, "ADHD & gifted."

Before I left, she gave me the name of a psychiatrist who would take my insurance—and give me meds.

The diagnosis has helped Kyle to be a little more under-standing when I forget we have plans or insist he buy me broc-coli only to let it rot in the bottom of the fridge. The medication helps me maintain my focus on work during the day so I can be more present with my family (there are four of us now) in the evenings. And couples therapy taught me that in a relationship, trying harder is usually a good thing.

People often say marriage is a compromise, but I see it more as learning to understand the other person's brain (and in my case, getting to know my own better, too). Kyle knows I need a few wildcard nights every week and I know he needs regular doses of my time and attention to feel emotionally secure. We've made it work with standing dates, including a "sacred" Thursday lunch.

I still mess up a lot, but I'm trying to get better every day. I've even become predictable in my own strange way. Last Thursday, I couldn't tear myself away from my desk and sent him a text from the shed I use as an office: "Running a few minutes late for lunch!"

He replied right away: "I know. I'm not going anywhere."

But let's not pretend that's my happy ending, because it's not. It's simply proof that I lucked out and the universe put an amazingly accommodating human in my path. The reality is that even the most thoughtful spouse can run out of patience when they feel ignored and abandoned—which is often still an issue when something shiny commands my attention. Most recently, it was my quest to find a disco ball for our chicken coop, and even I am annoyed by how on the nose that is.

Everything,
All the Time

You can do anything you put your mind to.

As an old Millennial—one of the oldest, born in 1982—this dictum was drilled into my head as a kid. I can't remember who said it to me, or when, but my best guess is "lots of people, very often." I'm sure it was also on a poster in my school guidance counselor's office, right next to the one featuring a terrified kitten hanging from a branch with the caption HANG IN THERE. By my sophomore year of high school, I had fully embraced this (totally ableist) motto as a personal mantra and I'd even put my own little spin on it: I wasn't just going to do *anything* I put my mind to, I was doing *everything* I put my mind to.

At the time, everything was this: In addition to my cashier job at Just For Feet (The World's Largest Athletic Shoe Store) next to the mall in Independence, Missouri, and my internship at a local country music station, I was involved in a handful of extracurricular activities, including student council, National Honor Society, drama club, chamber choir, dance team (we were called the Indianettes AND I'M SORRY), and marching band. And then there were the extra-extracurricular activities: getting to school early to host the closed-circuit morning news broadcast and, for a hot minute, running a radio station out of the cafeteria. It was mostly manageable. But five times a year, under the Friday night lights, things got a little tricky.

First up was singing. As a soprano in Touch of Class (classy, right?), I was expected to carry the highest notes in "The Star-Spangled Banner" before pass-off. Or the first kick? Or the . . . ass tap? (Whatever happens to start the sports ball game where the guys run into each other a lot and hurt their brains on purpose.) In the Red and White Brigade, I marched in formation during the halftime show, then handed my tenor sax to the sousaphone player and marked time while the rest of the problematically named Indianettes joined me on the field, where we'd then dance to a recording of whatever pop song was hot at the moment; "C'mon N' Ride It (The Train)" by the Quad City DJ's was perhaps the most memorable.

The adults in charge weren't great about hiding their frustration with how my zest for after-school life created some scheduling inconveniences for them and I can kind of understand why. I was all over the stadium during games—not with the band when our team scored and busy with the choir when the other Indianettes (yes, I cringe every time I type that) were doing the obligatory pregame prancing. But there wasn't much any of them could do about it. They *had* to share me, just like my divorced parents.

I made it through an entire school year without any major issues. But right before my junior year—when I was that nerd spending what was left of my summer at band camp *and* dance camp—both the Red and White Brigade and the Indianettes were scheduled to march in a local Labor Day parade. For the first time, I was forced to choose between band and dance.

The decision was easy. Missouri summers are brutal and often last well into October. There was no way in *hell* I was going to walk a mile in a thick, scratchy band uniform when I could dance the same route in some skimpy, sparkly spandex.

This is no big deal, I told myself as I walked into Ron P. Little's office, a glorified cinder-block closet near the entrance to the band room. I'd been busting my ass to make everything work and the Indianettes would miss me more than the Brigade would, so I figured he'd be cool with me skipping one off-site band performance.

I should have known better.

There were lots of words to describe Ron P. Little, but "cool" was not one of them. A trumpet player who loved high school band so much he made a career of it, he was very intense, regularly bellowing, "Tell me what gets things done!" in the middle of a rehearsal and expecting the entire band to reply with "Commitment!" in unison. His khaki pants also rode up a little at the crotch when he walked. So, yeah, I have no idea why I expected him to be cool about me breaking my commitment to his band, even for just one performance, *one* time.

Here's how the whole thing went down:

Me: Heeeeeeey, Mister Little. So, you probably know the drill team is scheduled for the Labor Day parade, too. Since there are only ten Indianettes, I'm going to march with them.

Him: . . .

Me: Also, remember that time I passed out when we were practicing in the sun? I wasn't even wearing my uniform then and if I have to wear that thing and walk while carrying *and* blowing into a giant piece of metal all at the same time—*in the sun,* in *this* weather—I'm gonna pass out again. That would be, like, so bad.

Him: So, what you're telling me, Emily, is that you're not committed to the Red and White Brigade. Do I have that right?

Me: No, I totally am. But I'm also committed to the Indianettes and there are ten of them and, like, sixty of us, so I figured they'd miss me more.

Obviously, I've paraphrased some of that conversation. It was 1998. Pre-Y2K. A bygone century. A whole other *millennium.* And I can't be expected to remember every little detail of our exchange, verbatim, decades later; I can't even remember if I ate breakfast this morning (though somehow I can still do the entire rap from TLC's "Waterfalls" and can karaoke pretty much any hit song from the nineties with a blindfold on). But I will never forget the exact words he said to (okay, yelled at) me after he slammed his hand down on his desk:

"You do everything and excel at nothing!"

It took me a few seconds to realize we were no longer bantering, but as soon as it hit me my face started to burn red hot and my eyes welled up with tears. Not because he'd hurt my feelings (he hadn't, really) but because confrontation with authority figures overwhelmed me. Plus, I knew right then and there that I was going to have to quit band. As much as I hated marching in the heat, getting to school at 6:00 a.m. (*-ish*) for practice multiple mornings a week, and lugging that giant fucking tenor sax case everywhere I went, I loved making music with other people; I was such a band nerd that I got chills every time we stepped onto the field.

But this wasn't something I could just forget. It would have made staying in band unbearable and it would have been all I thought about during rehearsals, performances, and competitions.

With one shitty comment—that was really inappropriate for a teacher to say to a student, even in the nineties—Mr. Little killed what little passion I had left for his program.

It crossed my mind for just a second that *not* quitting might give me some stick-it-to-the-man satisfaction. If I really wanted to, I could have stayed in band—remained *committed*—and become his worst nightmare. I could have purposely played the wrong notes and marched out of step and taken a big swig of my sugary gas station "cappuccino" right before blowing into my school-issued instrument. But I knew myself well enough to know that quitting really, really dramatically would be far more satisfying. Plus, if I was being honest, I was ready to move on to something else. I'd accomplished all the things I'd wanted to in band, and the new had long ago worn off. I kept doing it because I thought I was supposed to. Because I believed lots of people would be really disappointed in me if I casually gave it up. And because up until that day in that crappy little cinder-block office, I still had yet to experience the feelings of relief and possibility that come with quitting something that was no longer bringing me joy.

"Well, *now* I'm not committed to band anymore," I growled, trying really hard to hold back my tears and also to hit him where it hurt. "I quit."

Ron P. Little may have crossed a line when he told me I do everything and excel at nothing, but he wasn't entirely wrong, either. I didn't actually excel at much. Yes, I'd auditioned well enough to earn a coveted spot in chamber choir, but it wasn't because I was an amazing singer. I could read music and I wanted it so badly I trained my voice to hit the high notes by singing along to the title track from the *Phantom of the Opera* CD whenever I was alone in the janky Ford Probe I drove to and from school and my various jobs and internships. Straight As were pretty easy for me, but if I'd ever bothered to study—or just read the damn book, *any* book that had been assigned by an English teacher—I might have been at the very top of my class. My fellow Indianettes had nicknamed me "P.T." because, for some reason, it was impossible for me to do any choreography without also working in my infamous pelvic thrust. I had even been first-chair tenor saxophone in Ron P. Little's Wind Ensemble, my high school's top-tier concert band, but that's far less impressive when you learn there were only two tenor sax players in the whole school and the other guy just wasn't very good. In fact, the only two places I seemed to truly excel were theater and writing, though both could be attributed to natural talent—not strict adherence to practice.

But I was only in high school, and more importantly, I was having fun. I loved the thrill of a new activity, an internship I was probably underqualified for, a hectic Friday night, a fully booked schedule. I was doing what I could to make four long years at a rural Missouri high school bearable so I could get the hell out of there as soon as possible, while also trying to make enough money to keep myself in unfortunately low-cut Lucky Jeans and Doc Martens. Making a commitment to anything was simply not part of that plan. And I feel like I shouldn't have to point this out, but I was technically still a kid.

When I relayed the story of my encounter with Mr. Little to friends and family, everyone confirmed what I'd been thinking, too: Ron P. Little was a real big asshole. And that high school was the place for trying all the things, even all at the same time. And, hey, at least I was excelling at *that*.

I was lucky the school year hadn't yet started when Mr. Little and I had our little altercation, so I was able to fill the time I would have spent in band with another class. Except it wasn't really a class, since I somehow talked the principal into letting me do an independent study of my school's very unpopular Russian-language curriculum (spoiler alert: I did not excel there and I don't speak a word of Russian). Though I occasionally missed the act of playing music as part of an ensemble, band quickly became a distant memory. Besides, I had chamber choir to scratch my musical itch. I also got more involved in theater (or thea*tre*, as I obnoxiously spelled it back then), and by my senior year, I was drama club president as well as vice president of my class. Then there were my internships (yes, plural), my part-time job as a hostess at Steak & Ale, and, of course, the requisite high school partying.

As graduation loomed, more than one teacher stopped me in the hall to let me know how much potential I had. The backhanded compliments were usually followed by some teacherly wisdom spoken in more hushed tones:

"You need to focus more."

"I'd really like to see you follow through with something."

"Once you learn to harness your energy, you'll be unstoppable."

"Just *try harder*, Emily."

One teacher gifted me with an inscribed self-help book called *Don't Sweat the Small Stuff . . . and It's All Small Stuff* and I didn't even make it halfway through. I recently went back to look at the tattered offering I've been carrying around for more than twenty years—along with the guilt of never finishing it—and now I can see why I quit that, too. The chapters had titles like, "Make Peace with Imperfection," "Don't Interrupt Others or Finish Their Sentences," "Become More Patient," and "Allow Yourself to Be Bored." All things that are practically impossible for me.

I realize this is the point in the story where I might be expected to admit defeat . . . or at least exhaustion. And if I had a "normal" brain—or had I been the barely legal manic pixie dream girl in a coming-of-age rom-com—that might have happened. Staring down the rest of my life in the real world probably should have forced me to pick a passion, stick with it, and finally excel at something. (If I wanted to be precious about it, maybe I'd take up the old tenor sax in college and go on to become a true virtuoso.) But as much as I wanted to back then, I was never normal, and as far as I know, I wasn't anybody's dream girl, either.

Like my parents and teachers, I assumed I'd grow out of whatever it was that had me doing everything all the time. I'd go to college, pick a major (double major, of course), get some sort of journalism job, stay at said job for a reasonable amount of time, be financially stable by age thirty, get married, have kids, and become a slightly intimidating but well-loved media boss by forty. Because that's what adults do. And I did do some of that, though not in any sort of conventional way, and I never stayed in any one place very long. I went to college, then switched to one that never made me pick a major. It took me six years to graduate and I don't think I'll ever recover from that debt. I've worked in media for most of my career, too, but it's been an ever-changing combination of mostly free-lance jobs: lifestyle writer, copywriter, graphic designer, food stylist, branded content writer, commerce writer, recipe developer, social media consultant, editor, cookbook publicist, cocktail photographer—while also dabbling in interior design and teaching myself how to edit video and audio. My CV reads more like an IMDb profile of roles I've been typecast for than a true résumé. I've had two podcasts, five very different blogs (each with their own small but loyal following), and a few Etsy shops I shut down because I couldn't keep up with mailing product or managing inventory. I've hosted cooking competitions and crafting events in Kansas City and New York, and someone once paid me to cut her hair—which I'm 99 percent sure is illegal, considering I don't have a cosmetology license. For a while, I played tambourine and sang backup in a folksy Americana band. I even got married and had kids. (I could go on, but I compiled all the jobs and gigs I could remember in a CV at the back of the book for your reference . . . and mine.)

I wouldn't say I necessarily excel at any of it, but I don't need to—or want to. I'd get bored doing just one thing, or even three things, for the rest of my life. Plus, I'm as good as I need to be. My recipes, articles, and photos have been in glossy magazines and I've been quoted in publications I like to read. I've designed restaurant logos, billboards, and wedding invitations and, for years, I built beautiful websites for extra cash. When I was twenty-six, I wrote a cookbook for a major publisher, and not long after posting about my DIY kitchen renovation on one of my short-lived blogs, a big-name television producer relentlessly tried to get me to make a pilot for HGTV. I made a few demo reels before realizing I would get bored with my own TV show, too.

When I learned that my brain doesn't process the neurotransmitter dopamine the way other people's brains do and started to understand how ADHD affects women and girls, my self-inflicted chaos began to make so much sense. I'm still working on being more self-aware, but at least I no longer feel like I will (or should) grow out of anything. My truth is that I need new challenges, stressful situations, looming deadlines, and imminent gratification to keep my brain awake enough to get anything done. In many ways, my ADHD is a real asset. Because once I resolve to do something, I will hyperfocus on it until I decide I'm done—even, or especially, if it's outside my skill set when I begin.

My constant need for change makes domestic life a challenge, and nearly two years of lockdown certainly didn't help, but I'm committed, though my hyperfocus on a project often comes at the expense of family time. When Kyle gets frustrated that I'm always changing things—paint colors, light fixtures, the configuration of our entire home—but can't sit down on the couch with him, I try to remind him that tearing apart the house is a better way to feed the dopamine monster than packing up and moving. I've tried to talk him into demolishing a wall or renovating a bathroom with me, but he fears change as much as I crave it and would rather keep our house exactly the way it is, warped baseboards and all. Secretly, I'm fine with doing these things on my own because "once the brain train has left the station," as I like to say, there's no stopping me. Another set of hands would make things harder, but I don't tell him that part. Anyway, I'm too busy to have those conversations right now since I'm working my first full-time job in years, writing a book, parenting two small kids, and trying to talk myself out of starting my own lipstick line because the perfect shade of neon red doesn't yet exist.

I guess Ron P. Little was right about me all along. More than twenty years after he stood in his office and yelled "You do everything and excel at nothing!" I'm still doing everything and excelling at nothing. And I wouldn't want it any other way.

He was wrong about one thing, though: it's not commitment that gets things done; it's dopamine.

Undiagnosed

Sometimes, on snow days, after my little sister Jo and I came in from sledding, our mom would put the tiniest capful of peppermint schnapps in our hot chocolate. If Barb couldn't send us off to school, she could at least attempt to knock us out long enough for her to watch her favorite soap opera, *Guiding Light*, uninterrupted.

Now that I've lived through a pandemic with two small children—one of whom decided to stop napping on the very first day of lockdown—I guess I can empathize with Barb. A little. I'm not saying I endorse microdosing kids with cheap booze (or any booze), but the nineties were a different time, and she was a broke single mom doing the best she knew how to do. Plus, is a teensy-weensy bit of schnapps really any worse than, say, a big swig of NyQuil? I'd like to leave that one open for debate.

Still, whenever I bring up the snow days schnapps with Jo, she denies it ever happened—which means one of three things:

1. I am completely misremembering this. (Except I'm pretty sure that mouthwashy taste is still lingering in the back of my throat.)
2. Jo doesn't understand that it's way too late for CPS to come for us or send Barb to jail.
3. I'm the only one who got the schnapps because I'm just too much.

I was always too much for my mom.

"You're just like your father!" she would scream at me in my worst moments—complete meltdowns when our less-than-stellar financial situation made it impossible for me to do or have something I really wanted, fits of rage when Jo would sneak into my room and take something without asking. According to Barb, I generally acted like "a condescending little snot."

I wish I could say they were her worst moments, too. Worse than the yelling or the spanking, though, was when she didn't do anything at all. When I struggled—with keeping friends at school, avoiding bullies on the bus, missing my dad during the week—I mostly kept it to myself. Barb wasn't the most sympathetic parent in the world and I generally got the sense she didn't really like me. I mean, I knew she loved me—she told me as much—but she never seemed to enjoy my company. She was at her best as a mother when Jo and I were sick, and I think that's because sick kids don't really talk back. Also, they're extra snuggly. (To this day, Barb likes to remind me that I weaned myself and "rejected" her hugs by the time I turned one.)

I probably could have used a few capfuls of schnapps the night I decided to tell Barb what I'd barely figured out myself: there was something wrong with my brain.

I was ten and up later than any kid should be on a school night, but bedtime was always more of a suggestion than a rule for Jo and me—especially if I kept to myself in my room, which I was more than happy to do. It would still be a few years before I got a little TV in there, but I was usually pretty content doing some sort of project: sponge-painting the walls a deep red, making a collage from old magazines, drawing horses (I was really into horses back then, but too poor to be a true horse girl), cross-stitching, painting over the red with seven coats of baby blue, reading. Anything but homework. That spring, I'd also been sneaking into the bathroom to shave the blonde peach fuzz from my prepubescent legs with one of Barb's rusty disposable razors because no matter how much I reasoned and begged, she was dead set on me waiting until my eleventh birthday to shave.

This was different from arguing over rules, though; I was asking for something intangible and it made me anxious. Would she even take me seriously? I was smart, got good grades, and teachers were always telling her what a wonderful—if eager and chatty—student I was. But it wasn't the school part of my brain that was broken. It was something else, something I needed an adult to handle and, hopefully, fix.

I waited for a commercial break to make my move.

"I need help," I said to her permed blonde hair over the back of the wood glider she liked to sit in while watching her shows. She turned her head about ninety degrees and gave me just enough side-eye to let me know she was half-listening. "I think there might be something wrong with my brain."

"Okay?"

I couldn't quite tell from the tone of her "okay" whether she expected further explanation or just thought I was being dramatic. Like my father. But I seemed to have her attention for a minute, so I wanted to choose my words carefully.

Where to start, though? I saw other kids my age making friends more easily and doing their homework when they were supposed to. Other kids my age went to sleep at a decent hour and got out of bed in the morning when it was time to get ready for school. Other kids my age could catch a ball, keep their backpacks clean, eat mashed potatoes without gagging, and wear tights without scratching their legs until they bled. And I was certain that most other kids my age didn't feel rage so intense that it seemed like it might burst out of their chests.

"Other kids don't get as angry as I do," I offered. My anger issues weren't news to her, so I started there.

"Well, what do you want me to do about it?"

"I don't know," I said, though I did know. I wanted her to do something, anything, first. To have already done something. To tell me we'd figure it out. To be the mom. "Maybe I should see a counselor?"

"Okay," she told me as she turned back to *L.A. Law.* "We can talk about it later."

But we never did.

I could be really pissed at Barb, and back then I was, for lots of things. So pissed, in fact, that when I was sixteen and my dad bought a little beige split level close to my high school, I couldn't move into his mostly finished basement quickly enough—or yell at her loudly enough as I shoved as much as I could fit into my red Ford Probe.

These days, I'm better at managing my anger. One way I do that is by putting things in perspective. For example, I try to be grateful that it was "just" ADHD that my mom completely ignored. Because if it had been a brain tumor, I'd definitely be dead by now.

Seventeen
Little Stories
Because I'm on My Period So My
Meds Aren't Working As Well As
They Should and My Kids Have Colds
and I'm Exhausted from My Day Job,
So I Can't Focus Enough to Write
One Long Essay Right Now

1. Talented, but Not Quite Gifted

In elementary school, my teachers constantly told my parents and me how smart and talented I was. But according to an entrance exam I took multiple times, I wasn't *quite* smart enough to test into TAG, my district's Talented and Gifted program. At age forty, I learned from an ADHD coach that TAG programs, sometimes also called G/T or GATE, are not status clubs for the smartest kids but, in fact, are supposed to be for kids like me, who would benefit from more creative, challenging, hands-on education.

2. They're All Going to Laugh at You

When I was eight, I was a candle lighter in my cousin's big, fat nineties wedding. My attire consisted of a custom-made white satin dress with very puffy sleeves (to match the bride's puffier lace sleeves), opaque white tights, and white patent leather Mary Janes. As we were getting dressed for the ceremony, I cried to my mom, aunts, and grandma because the tights were just so itchy I couldn't stand it and they all told me to suck it up. At the reception, I scratched the sides of my legs so intensely that rivers of blood ran down my legs, *Carrie* style.

3. Middle Sister

For the first eleven years of my life, I was the big sister, but just barely, because my little sister, Jo, is only fifteen months younger. In 1993, we met our half-sister Heather, from my dad's first marriage. She's ten years older than I am, and though we'd known of her existence, my dad had been out of touch with her since before I was born. I only know some of the story and it's not mine to tell, but imagine my disappointment when I sent my spit off to 23andMe at age thirty-eight and didn't find any more long-lost siblings.

4. The Front Row

I was the girl who always sat in the front row—until my ninth-grade chemistry teacher told me I asked too many questions. I eventually made my way back to the front row, but it took a long time for me to feel comfortable there again. And I still have to work really hard to not speak up too much in meetings.

5. The Girl with the Tingly Tongue

Until I was in the sixth grade, I thought a blow job was something you did to a car, like a lube job or a brake job. Later, in high school, when I attempted to give my first blow job, I asked the guy to put on a condom. He only had the kind with spermicide. I did not give a blow job for a long time after that.

6. Two Become One

When I was fifteen, I fantasized about losing (which is really the worst term because it's not something you misplace) my virginity to the Spice Girls' song "2 Become 1." In retrospect, my fantasies weren't very sexy, and I didn't have anyone particular in mind for the job, but none of that was really the point.

Two years later, I was nowhere close to finding the other half of any fuzzy, sexy math equation, and as high school graduation loomed, I decided to just get it over with. The lucky guy? A twenty-something sales guy at the shoe store where I worked as a cashier. We did it in his gross bed at his gross apartment behind the gross bowling alley behind the mall. There was no Spice Girls soundtrack. There was no music at all.

7. Wipeout

Before Kelly and Mark, and Kelly and Ryan before them, and Kelly and Michael before *them*, there was Kelly and Regis. But before Kelly and Regis, there was Regis and Kathie Lee. And when Kathie Lee left *Live! With Regis and Kathie Lee* in the year 2000, ABC held open auditions for her replacement. With a few years of high school theater and a couple of broadcasting classes under my belt, I threw myself into the ring. After spending at least six hours in a greenroom with thirty or so other people who were far more qualified to, you know, cohost a daily national talk show, they finally called my name. As I confidently strutted my Express-clad self onto the makeshift set, the high heel of my black leather Nine West boot hit the linoleum floor at just the right angle to slip out from under me and I wiped out in front of the producers—which I'm sure was the only reason I didn't get the job.

8. Easy A

When I was in college (before the advent of Google Docs and ubiquitous Wi-Fi), I managed to convince a professor I'd turned in a paper that I never wrote. He said, "Oh, yeah! I remember that. It was good!" A few days later, I learned he gave me an A minus and, to be honest, I was a little miffed about the minus.

9. A Walk to Remember

I used to babysit for a family on the Upper East Side and in addition to my hourly fee and the fifty dollars they left on a pile of delivery menus, they always gave me cab fare to get home. Because I was a broke college student, I usually pocketed the cash and walked or took the subway. If I walked, I'd use that time to call my parents or my sister back in the Midwest.

One Saturday night, my mom was doing her whole worried song and dance because I was out on the streets alone after dark. As I was rolling my eyes to no one and explaining to her that New York City is so much safer than Kansas City, I heard a man say, "Tell her you're with me and you're fine."

I looked to my right and it was . . . that guy from the sitcom *Murphy Brown*! I couldn't remember his name and told him as much, but I did remember that my mom was a huge fan of the show, so after asking his permission, I handed my phone to Jay Thomas!

He talked to her as he walked me from 68th Street all the way to my left turn in the East Village. *The whole time.* Jay Thomas made small talk with my mom and walked me home for at least fifty blocks. And that's the end of my story about Jay Thomas because he wasn't a creep. A decade after that, a much more famous man threatened to destroy my life. He wasn't a creep either, but I'll tell you more about that later.

10. Poop Chute

In 2004, I wrote an article about colonic irrigation that included the line "My ass had officially lost its virginity" (investigative journalism at its finest!). My dad found it after googling my name and, as far as I understand, hasn't read anything I've written since then.

(Dad, if you hoped this book might be less uncomfortable than anything I've written for the internet, I probably already lost you at the blow job. But, if by some miracle, you managed to power through, you should probably take a little break now. Maybe go get a beer. Also be sure to skip the following essays: "Street Drugs," "A Breakup Story," "No, I Will Not Shut Up About My Abortion," "Tramp Stamp," "Things I've Forgotten and Things I Don't Think I'll Ever Forget," and "Yes, I Have a Body.")

11. The Pep Talk

While I was still in college, I worked at a nonprofit in New York City. I had been hired as an assistant grant writer, but I really wanted to launch a blog and produce newsletters instead. When the communications director left, I made a case for moving me into the communications department and I got the job (though at the "associate" level, right where I belonged). One afternoon, the executive director called me into his office and told me I needed to be less direct and to "soften my approach" when requesting things from my coworkers. "Just be nicer, more polite," he advised. "Instead of telling people you 'need' something, say, 'may I please have this when it's convenient for you?'" I quit soon after, but I probably would have done that anyway.

12. The Phone Call

At the end of 2009, I decided I would quit drinking for a while—six months, maybe a year. I wanted to make sure I wasn't an alcoholic. I also wanted to try dating without my go-to social lubricant, figuring I could someday write a funny book about my awkward attempts at sober dating. I'd had my first drink long before I'd had my first real date and didn't really know how to interact with men without a drink in my hand (or a few in my system).

As part of my research, I was reading Caroline Knapp's beautiful memoir, *Drinking: A Love Story*, about her relationship with alcohol (among other things). In one scene, she's working as the lifestyle editor of a Boston newspaper when the man who would become her life partner calls her work phone—a *landline*—to ask her out on a date. When I read that passage, I thought, *Well, that is a thing that will never happen to me.* It was 2010 and I'd been meeting men online for a decade already, so I was confident about that fact. I happened to be working as a lifestyle editor of a local digital publication, and though I did have a landline at my desk, I only used it on the rare occasion I needed to call someone for a story *and* I didn't want whoever I was calling to be in possession of my cell phone number.

A week later, a contributor to the site I'd met recently at a concert called my work phone to ask me out on a date; he was hoping I was free that night. I turned him down because I had a big magazine pitch due the next morning, but I called him later (from my cell phone, of course) and suggested we go out the following week.

The man was Kyle.

13. Reading Incomprehension

Four years after six years of college, I signed up to take the GRE. I had decided I wanted to go to grad school but only because I had what seemed like a brilliant idea for a novel and I knew there was no way I'd be able to finish it without the accountability of an MFA program. Unfortunately, I wasn't able to complete the reading comprehension portion of the test before the time was up, so I rejected my score at the end.

14. My Design ADD

Eight years before I was diagnosed with ADHD, I wrote an article for AOL's now-defunct home decor site about my desire to constantly change things in my apartment. I titled it "My Design ADD."

15. The Handshake

On my wedding day, my dad walked up to the man who would be my husband in T-minus ninety minutes and offered his hand along with an ominous, "Well, I guess you know what you're getting into." Reader, he did not.

16. Fangirl

"You don't *really* need to sleep with a fan," Kyle would tell me every time we were in a hotel or Airbnb and I couldn't sleep because, well, I didn't have a fan. "You just think you do. You've trained yourself to think you need one."

When I was being evaluated for ADHD, the psychologist and I were discussing some of my quirks and she asked, "I bet you have to sleep with a fan on, too?"

17. It's Not a Sex Swing

A month or two into my family's three-week Covid lockdown, my senses were completely overwhelmed with touch, sound, and the mess that seemed to regenerate no matter how much I tried to stay on top of it. Desperate for a way to escape the chaos, I installed an adult-size sensory swing in the one place that was all mine: my ad hoc home office. There wasn't really space for the swing in the cozy little attic room with its dramatically sloped ceilings, but I made it work because I had to. Every time I climbed into my stretchy fabric cocoon, I prayed to the Flying Spaghetti Monster that the screws would hold and I wouldn't fall to my death and bring a hundred-year-old beam down with me.

Once I started taking Zoom meetings, I learned that even when I removed the swing—which was affixed to the bracket with a carabiner—there was no angle from which I could conceal the giant steel loop bolted to the low ceiling behind me. For months, every time I signed in to a meeting, I preempted any possible speculation by pointing up to (and therefore pointing out) the heavy-duty hardware and announcing, "It's not a sex swing! It's a yoga swing!" I'm so clearly not a person who does yoga, but that was much easier to explain than a sensory swing. I guess a sex swing wouldn't have needed much explanation either.

A Case of the Mondays

No one bats an eye when I rattle off a list of all the odd jobs I've held, including but not limited to fragrance model ("Would you like to try some Tommy Girl?"), nanny, political organizer, and ghostwriter of a self-help book on how to snag a man and get a ring in a ridiculously short window of time. But then I get to the part about training to be a stockbroker and people start demanding explanations.

I moved to New York City two months after I graduated high school with big dreams of becoming a Broadway actress or *SNL* cast member, though I would have gladly settled for MTV VJ if that opportunity called. Within a year, I was already way off track, working as an assistant to Arianna, a very tall stockbroker with very long hair. She had converted a studio apartment in Manhattan's financial district to a sunny private office and my desk was tucked into a dark corner close to the kitchenette.

It was supposed to be a summer job to help me recover financially from my first year of college in the city, but

39

Arianna—likely desperate to hold onto someone who knew her way around a computer—convinced me to stay. The way she sold it to me was this: I'd train under her and learn everything there was to know about trading and then my next job would (naturally) be as a talking head on MSNBC. *Naturally.*

"Once you understand the stock market, it'll be so easy for you to get a job as a business reporter or financial analyst," she told me. "I'll teach you everything you need to know in a year or two."

It was a far cry from Studio 8H or even Carson Daly's Times Square *Total Request Live* perch, but I figured it was, at least, a step in the right direction. Also, I was penniless.

"I'll work around your class schedule, too," she offered. "But try to take as many night classes as you can."

She had to have known I was never going to do anything in finance because every Friday I gladly accepted a handwritten check for exactly three hundred dollars. And every Monday, I came back for more.

I wish I could say my paychecks were so small because Arianna was withholding taxes or social security or a measly contribution to my health coverage, but nope; she was simply paying me $7.50 an hour. On the other hand, she did buy us Starbucks and fancy salads every day *and* she reliably handed me legal tender once a week, so it felt like an okay-enough deal at the time. I wasn't really learning anything because I spent most of my days scheduling client calls, fetching our caffeine and greens, delivering documents to old white men in dark suits, and picking up her dry cleaning (slim cigarette pants and oxford shirts with exaggerated collars), with the occasional spreadsheet task thrown in.

But those salads were really nice.

One Monday, after a particularly unfulfilling shift "on Wall Street" (but really Rector Street), my second cousin and his girlfriend invited me over for gin and tonics. I didn't know them well, and I was tired after eight hours of errands in Manhattan followed by a night class in Brooklyn, but I couldn't exactly afford to buy my own booze. Also, I was only nineteen. Some time with family (even family I didn't know very well) could do me good. I hopped on the train and headed to Astoria.

I'd never had gin and tonic before and it only took about half of one to admit to my hosts—but mostly to myself—how I really felt about my work situation. And once I started saying it, I couldn't stop.

"I hate it so fucking much."

"I hate it *so* fucking much."

"I hate it SO FUCKING MUCH!"

(Two decades later, me drunkenly repeating myself is a predictable habit that mostly just annoys my husband, but that night, it was proof of my passion. An emphasis on injustice!)

"Then why don't you just quit?" my cousin's girlfriend asked, as if quitting a job was no big deal. As if I had a backup plan. As if I had any money in the bank. She made four times as much as I was making working as a nanny on the Upper East Side. And she had legit benefits—good ones—*plus* daily Starbucks and fancy salads.

"I can definitely get you some babysitting work," she promised. "Twenty bucks an hour. Cash."

Wait a minute. I could just . . . quit? A job? By then, I knew the joy of quitting. I'd done my fair share of enthusiastically committing to something only to decide shortly thereafter that it wasn't a good fit (see: regular consumption of vegetables, flossing, the saxophone, the bassoon, putting away my clean laundry, and a belly button piercing that was never not infected, to name a few). But it never occurred to me to just up and quit a *job*. A job was serious business. My dad had been at his for at least fifteen years. His dad had the same one his entire life. Suddenly quitting a job was something people only did in movies—some Jerry Maguire shit. Plus, wouldn't it, like, go on my permanent record?

Unfortunately, once the idea was in my head, that was it. Even though I was broke, and some part of my brain understood that quitting my job without another one lined up was a terrible idea, I *had* to quit. And I had to quit immediately.

While I was new to quitting a job, the sensation to make it happen right away was nothing new. It's pretty much how I ended up in New York a year earlier with no job, no apartment, and no money to my name. At just nineteen, I already had a history of quickly making a decision, then feeling like if I didn't act on it in that moment I might die of anticipation. I'd been called "impulsive" by parents, grandparents, and teachers, been told by other adults that I "didn't think things through." What nobody seemed to get was that I *did* think things through, I just happened to do it really quickly—efficiently, if you will—and that the more I thought about something, the more I had to have or do it, even if "it" wasn't the most rational thing. But I could rationalize anything if I wanted it badly enough and I maintained that I was just an impassioned young person with good instincts who didn't want to have any regrets. You can't pay bills with no regrets, but that was a problem for another day (like one of the many days throughout that decade that Sprint would threaten to shut off my cell phone for nonpayment).

I knew enough about the real world to understand that quitting without notice was bad form, but I also knew I couldn't handle another two weeks in that alcove studio-turned-office with its parquet floors, windowless bathroom, and chintzy kitchenette. Over the course of one hour and just as many gin and tonics, quitting had become the *only* option, yet the idea of delivering the news to Arianna in the morning filled me with anxiety. Because, of all the things I'd tried to avoid in my nineteen years, Confrontation with Authority Figures was up there with pregnancy, group sports, and bedbugs. The encounters always left me feeling overwhelmed, flustered, and fragile. And often in tears.

Then I remembered I had a key! Problem. Solved. I could sneak in, take my stuff, and leave a note—very much like the breakup Post-It Berger would leave for Carrie in *Sex and the City* two years later. So I choked down one more gin and tonic, thanked my cousin and his girlfriend for the liquid courage, and got back on the train headed toward lower Manhattan.

Entering the building at night felt criminal, which was honestly kind of thrilling. But I wasn't a criminal—just a teenage girl who didn't have the guts to quit her shitty job in person.

I crept through the lobby as if someone were watching me. (No one was watching me.) I let myself into the office and collected the tuxedo-style blazer I'd been instructed to buy with my first paycheck in case an important client ever popped by unexpectedly. It still had the tags, and I wondered if Century 21 would let me return it so I'd have some cash. Then I grabbed a piece of copy paper from the printer and wrote: "I'm so sorry. I can't do this job anymore. I don't want to be a stockbroker. I hope you don't hate me.—Emily." (See? I told you it was a lot like Berger's Post-It.)

I made a point of locking the door handle on my way out—then telling myself out loud that I had locked it—and practically skipped back to the subway station. After four soulless months, I was finally free!

The problem with freedom, though, is that it's often followed by panic. Leaving with no notice was a dick move toward a boss who'd always treated me kindly, even if the job sucked (which it sure as shit did). The chances of interacting with Arianna ever again were slim—I'd never need a professional reference from a *stockbroker*—but people-pleasing is part of the Millennial DNA and I didn't want her to hate me. Also, from a financial standpoint, I was totally screwed. I had no job, no plan, no savings, and, obviously, no trust fund (pretty sure trust funds don't exist where I come from). My last paycheck hadn't yet cleared my bank account and I barely had enough cash to buy myself a bodega coffee the next morning. A fancy salad was a pipe dream.

As the half-empty subway car rattled its way a few stops uptown, I reminded myself that I had made the right decision.

It was a good thing that would only feel icky for a minute. And I knew I'd figure it out; even back then, "figuring shit out" was one of my superpowers. It could also be called me "scrambling to clean up my own messes," but somehow things were always okay enough in the end.

By the time I got home, I was feeling better. Home that year was a room on the shared floor of a West Village townhouse, where I lived rent free in exchange for working three nights a week at the church next door. My job was to let people into different spaces for twelve-step meetings and then lock up the building at night. I also did what I'd now consider really bad social work, attempting to help people who came in off the streets high, hungry, or both.

This living arrangement was something else I'd "figured out" about six months after moving to the city. It was a ridiculously sweet deal, despite the other occupants of my apartment being more like curmudgeonly neighbors than roommates. One was the church handyman, whose room was at the end of the hall opposite mine and whose age was somewhere between forty and eighty years old—I could never quite tell because he'd been seriously electrocuted twice and it had burned part of his face and the entire top of his head, rendering him bald and brutally scarred. My other roommate was a thirtysomething chef whose deal was similar to mine. She worked the nights I didn't and I was sure she hated me for many reasons, not least of which was that I was constantly using a dial-up connection to get online and then forgetting to sign off, which meant no one could call in or out of the apartment's sole phone. It wasn't a problem for me since I had a cell phone, but our shared landline was her only form of telephonic communication.

Every time I stepped out of my room, I felt like I was about to get into trouble for something. Still, I was quite content sharing a hallway, bathroom, and kitchen (there was no living room) with these weirdos who maybe definitely hated me. I didn't need them to like me because I had my very own big, bright space with exposed brick and two windows overlooking West 4th Street. And it was *free*. Well, it wasn't exactly free, but it didn't require me to manage any money or commute more than fifty feet to at least one of my jobs, which was honestly better than free . . . I think.

I paced around my big free-ish bedroom, trying to figure out what to do with all the I-just-quit-my-job energy coursing through me. It was too late to call my cousin's girlfriend and texting wasn't really a thing yet, so I signed into AOL to send her an email. I let her know everything had gone smoothly but that I'd be in touch ASAP about that babysitting work. (Translation: "I need money. Bad.")

I considered emailing my dad to tell him I might need to borrow a few hundred dollars ("Just one more time!") to hold me over until I found a new job, but I decided that uncomfortable exchange could wait another twelve hours. The whole night had been an emotional roller coaster and I crawled into bed exhausted and giddy at the thought of sleeping in as late as I wanted on a Tuesday.

Not enough hours later, I woke to the sound of someone pounding on my bedroom door. I could tell it was the chef who hated me by her frenetic knock; the few times the handyman knocked, he'd employed a much more timid tap. I looked at my clock. It wasn't even nine yet. Had I forgotten to turn off the bathroom light? Left stinky leftovers in the fridge too long? Neither warranted such a rude awakening on my first weekday to sleep in, so I didn't respond. If she thought I was at work, she'd eventually go away (that, or I'd learn she was a snooper). But she didn't stop. She kept banging. Then she started yelling.

"Emily! Emily! Are you in there? Emily? Answer me if you're in there!"

I begrudgingly forced myself out of bed and opened the door, but before I had a chance to tell her to piss off, her entire body relaxed with an exasperated, "Oh, thank God!" Then she told me to turn on my TV because a plane had just crashed into the World Trade Center.

Well, this is more interesting than going into that soul-sucking office, I thought as I prepared to spend the rest of the day glued to my thirteen-inch screen. Because like everyone else in the world, I assumed it was an accident.

Each channel I tried was a mess of gray static, so the chef, the handyman, and I—along with everyone else in Manhattan—ran outside to watch with our own eyes what was happening. We'd hardly had time to process what *was* actually happening when the second plane hit. People started screaming, and maybe I did, too, I don't remember. Mostly, we just stood there because there was nothing else to do and nowhere to go. I hated that feeling. I was like a pot about to boil over and I needed something—anything!—to do with all of that nervous energy.

At some point I went back to my room to change out of my pajamas and into real clothes, because, though I had no idea what I would do next, I knew I couldn't do nothing.

As I swapped my ridiculous orange striped onesie for more functional jeans and a T-shirt, it occurred to me that my family had no clue I'd already quit my "new" job. For all they knew of the city's geography, it could have been right next to the towers. Arianna's office happened to be a few blocks south of what would soon come to be known as Ground Zero, and on a beautiful day like that one was supposed to be, I most certainly would have taken the E train from West 4th Street to the World Trade Center station and walked the rest of the way—even if I was running late. And I was *always* running late.

I grabbed my phone and, on the way downstairs, tried to call my dad, then my mom, then my sister Jo, but I couldn't get through to any of them. There was no ringing on my end, just dead air. I kept trying even after neighbors who had gone inside to make their own calls came back out to report that landlines weren't working, either.

Then the South Tower fell. It would be another half hour before the North Tower collapsed, too, but it was like it all happened at the same time. Everything was happening. Everything was collapsing. The sky was falling. The world, as I had known it, was ending. And I was just standing there.

When the ghost people started to spill onto my block from the cloud of dust, I felt a strange sense of relief—not only because I saw survivors, but also because finally there was something for me to *do*.

The chef, the handyman, the pastor, and I opened up the big, red sanctuary doors and offered people what we could: a chair, a bottle of water, a granola bar from the church's food pantry, towels and T-shirts we always had on hand for the men who would wander in from the nearby shelter. And from our own closets: any comfortable shoes we could spare because most people who were lucky enough to make it home that day had to walk.

I don't know how many times I went back and forth between the church and my room to pee, to change into cleaner clothes, to find another pair of shoes I was willing to part with, to make sure my windows were shut—though it was too late and everything I owned was already covered in ash that was undoubtedly some combination of buildings and bodies. On one of those trips upstairs, I caught a glimpse of my dust-covered computer. *Had I signed off the night before?* I didn't remember signing off. But there was no way I was still connected to the internet . . . *right?* I wiggled my mouse hoping for a miracle, and there it was: an active AOL window. And I had mail. Of course I had mail.

I hadn't cried all day, but when I sat down to write back to my dad—to tell him that I was alive and that (surprise!) I'd quit my awful job the night before so I was very much not on my way to work when the planes flew into the buildings—the tears finally came. It was the first time I was able to think about what had happened, and what hadn't happened (at least not to me), and what could have happened if I hadn't made such a seemingly irresponsible, impulsive decision.

Obviously, there's no real way to know how things would have gone for me had I decided to give Arianna two weeks' notice instead of quitting on a gin-fueled whim, but it's safe to say I would have tried to exit the World Trade Center subway station right around the time the first plane hit. And because I thrive in emergency situations I might have tried to stick around to see if I could help. Instead, because I have what a doctor would later call "problems with impulse control," my story didn't end the way so many others' did that day. And because I'm easily distracted, I was in a place to send some families, including my own, a little good news at a dark and scary time.

I waited for the little woosh that confirmed my email would make it all the way to my dad's computer in Missouri, then I went back down to the church. The sanctuary was still packed because people kept showing up. Bankers, janitors, food service workers, bus drivers, students.

The one thing we all had in common (other than being covered in dust and existing in some state of shock) is that we had all been trying to reach loved ones by phone and none of us could.

"Just your name, and the email address of the person you want me to contact," I said as I walked around with a little notebook. "That's it. Nothing else." I felt a little bit like an asshole, but I was on a mission (finally!).

Not everybody had a relative with an email address, at least not one they knew off the top of their heads. But I filled a few small pages and each time I did, I went back upstairs and plugged the info into a little template.

Subject: [INSERT NAME OF DUST-COVERED PERSON HERE] Is Okay

Body: "I'm writing on behalf of your kid/parent/ sibling/partner/roommate who is still alive. They stopped at Washington Square United Methodist Church in the West Village and they're working on getting home now."

When I was done sending those emails, I wrote one more. It was to Arianna, to make sure she was okay, too. Since she always arrived at the office by eight, I knew she'd seen my note, so I didn't bother mentioning it (successfully avoiding confrontation yet again, I hoped).

She got back to me the evening of September 12. She was fine, physically, but had to evacuate the building after the first tower fell. I really wanted to reply and ask if she hated me for the way I quit, but instead I wrote, "I'm so glad you're safe."

Lipstick Is the Only Makeup You Can Put On in Public

When I was two months shy of my sixteenth birthday I drove myself to my Grandma Freda's wake. I only had my learner's permit and wasn't supposed to be behind the wheel without a licensed driver in the car, but my mom had let me make a few short trips on my own before. (There were a few she didn't know about, too.) When Grandma Freda died, Barb was too distraught to care about much else. I don't remember how she got to the funeral home, but I know it wasn't in her own car, because I was driving it. Alone.

Grandma Freda was frugal and generous and flamboyant and religious and racist as fuck. Born and raised one of nine children in Louisville, Kentucky, she was only fourteen years old at the start of the Great Depression.

She made perfectly chalky peanut butter fudge and reused the plastic jars for "raisin juice"—raisins soaked in tap water and, yes, it was as disgusting as it sounds. When we ate at buffets, she'd wrap fried chicken legs in paper napkins and stick them in her purse for later. She smoked for most of her life (it was emphysema that got her in the end) but was afraid of her microwave and put a plastic tray in front of her feet when she watched TV in bed to block the radiation. Her shower was jam-packed with clothes and I still have no idea how, or how often, she bathed, but she never smelled bad—just vaguely of vintage Avon. She put shredded cheese in her instant ramen and it was amazing, and whenever Jo and I would eat it on her sofa, which she called "the divan," she'd cover both "the divan" and the floor in front of it with vinyl tablecloths. Any time anyone asked, and sometimes when they didn't, she'd give amazing foot rubs—with lotion!—on that couch. She only put a small towel on her lap for those, though.

Grandma Freda stopped driving long before I was born. She quit after my grandfather died and said driving made her too sad because "we had some of our best times in the car." Apparently, they also enjoyed motel rooms; Grandpa William's fatal heart attack came while they were getting biblical during a vacation in Arkansas.

A few years after becoming a widow, she converted to a Sabbatarian church not unlike the Seventh-Day Adventists. Though she'd lived a mostly secular life, she'd been so moved by a television evangelist in Texas named Garner Ted Armstrong that she started going to a franchise of his Saturday church in Kansas City. (That plastic tray couldn't block the word of God, I guess.) My mom followed suit after my parents divorced and then Jo and I became the only kids we knew whose family didn't celebrate Christmas. Or Halloween. Or

Easter. (Safe to say my upbringing lacked diversity.) Luckily, my dad didn't stray too far from the Methodist Church after the split and he made sure we had anachronistically conventional holidays. Well, except that one year he didn't have money to buy us costumes, so we were bed-sheet ghosts and one of us had to be the Budweiser ghost. I can't remember which one of us ended up covered head to toe in Budweiser logos (save for the cut-out eye holes), but does it really matter *which* of your elementary-aged kids is wearing that thing?

I've still never gotten over Grandma Freda throwing away my dad's black Fleetwood Mac tour T-shirt I'd worn home from a weekend at his place. When I asked if she knew where it was, she told me it went out with the trash because it was "of the Devil." I wondered if she thought the same about my dad.

Her white hair was always perfectly coiffed and she never went anywhere without her bright pink or orange lipstick—which she kept in her purse with a little clip-on mirror for touch-ups.

"Lipstick is the only makeup you can put on in public," she would tell me.

She plucked her "whiskers" in front of the window and liked to remind all the women in the family that she weighed a hundred and nineteen pounds when she got married. (She also regularly told my mom and aunts that "Daddy doesn't like fat girls.") When I started wearing makeup, she told me I wore too much eyeliner. In hindsight, she wasn't wrong about that. (It was the nineties. My eyeliner was purposely thicker than my eyebrows.) One time, she made me poop into a paper grocery bag when the water in our house was shut off for repairs.

The independent living facility where Grandma Freda lived often invited residents' grandkids in to put on talent shows. Jo and I were regulars and once performed to New Kids on the Block. And when I say "performed," I mean we bouncy squatted and badly lip-synced our way through all four minutes and sixteen seconds of "Hangin' Tough." The next day, the building was abuzz with talk of the two little girls who had suggestively danced to such filthy lyrics. There *were* no filthy lyrics, but somehow the septuagenarians had heard "We're gonna put you in a trance with a funky song," and believed they'd heard F-bombs. "Fucky songs" really doesn't have much of a ring to it, and I recognized that even as an awkward, gap-toothed seven-year-old. Grandma Freda did, too, and she defended us against those old biddies until the day she died.

"Don't you worry about them," she assured us. "They're just grumpy old folks with bad ears."

Jo and I were never invited to perform at another talent show after that.

My grandmother gave freely—both her worldly belongings and her advice—but it's the advice I remember most.

In addition to the rule about lipstick, there was the weird-but-okay stuff:

"Sleep without underwear so you can air out *down there*."

And:

"Always wash your hands first thing in the morning
because you never know where they go at night."

The infuriating stuff:

"Always sacrifice comfort for beauty."

Then there's the truly awful stuff that's *too* awful to repeat
but I'm going to do it anyway because it's important to acknowledge that people can grow up hearing this stuff and not turn
out to be racist insurrectionist fucks:

"Don't look at Black people the wrong way or they'll
shootcha."

Grandma Freda was deeply flawed. She also loved us
fiercely. After my parents divorced, she took care of Jo and me
when my mom couldn't—which was fairly often.

I prided myself in being nothing like Grandma Freda. I
eschewed raisins, microwaved everything else, didn't really
believe in God or the Devil, wasn't afraid of Black people, and
was already well on my way to being an obnoxious little femi-
nist warrior. Sure, I liked my eyeliner, but I loudly rejected her
notion of sacrificing comfort for beauty, and when I was thirteen, I sat on her divan and hand-wrote a letter to the CEO of
Lane Bryant complaining about their size 10 models.

Because I had no filter, I had a counterargument to nearly
everything Grandma Freda said—even if she was never really

arguing in the first place. An uncle regularly joked that I "gave her hell." My mom accused me of having no respect for my elders. I was satisfied by the idea that I was standing up for what I knew was right and I'd like to think there was some part of my grandmother that wanted that for me, too.

As I drove to her wake—going exactly three miles over the speed limit to not appear suspiciously slow—I was overcome with guilt. I *had* given her hell for most of my nearly sixteen years on earth. And if not respecting someone's backward-ass beliefs meant I didn't respect the people who had them, well, I guess I didn't respect my elders, either.

I tried to make myself small at the funeral home. *Don't argue with anyone and don't make a scene*, I kept thinking. When I cried, I did it quietly. When her weird church friends tried to comfort me with talk of Jesus coming back (because I guess one time wasn't enough), I didn't roll my eyes. But when I finally made my way to her casket, I could feel myself starting to lose control. Not just because I felt guilty for being so unkind to her while she was still alive, but also because, stuffed into that satin-lined mahogany box, my Grandma Freda didn't look anything like my Grandma Freda. She was wearing a bubblegum-pink jacket dress I'd seen her wear to church and someone at the funeral home had done an okay job roller-setting her bright-white hair. But her face was all wrong. And it wasn't her stiff, gray skin that bothered me.

"Why didn't anybody tell them to put her lipstick on?!" I blurted out to anyone and everyone who happened to be behind me—which was practically everyone in attendance. And once

I opened my mouth, everything else spilled out of me, too. My crying turned audible, and as the tears poured from my eyes, they took some of that black eyeliner Grandma Freda hated so much along with them.

Barb told me to settle down. A few of the weird church people looked at me with pity. Jo's eyes got really big, like she knew what I was going to do before I did.

I didn't want to touch a dead body, I swear. And technically, I didn't, at least not with my bare hands. But even back then, I didn't believe in any sort of afterlife, so as far as I was concerned, this was Grandma Freda's final public appearance. And even if I had it all wrong, there's no way in hell—or whatever whole-earth heavenly Resurrection that Texas televangelist promised her—she'd want to show up at her version of the pearly gates without her lipstick on.

So, I did what absolutely no normal fifteen-year-old would do and I reached into my purse, pulled out a tube of Revlon, and twisted the base to reveal the rounded tip of my bright reddish-orange lipstick. I had to stand on my tippy toes to lean far enough into the casket to get a precise application and it certainly wasn't my best work—embalmed lips have absolutely no give—but it's what she would have wanted from me.

Maybe I'd picked up a few things from Grandma Freda after all. And the world is a slightly better place because it wasn't the racist stuff.

Why I Never Responded to Your Text

Because when I saw the preview pop up I could tell you were asking me a question and Kyle was trying to explain to me why we didn't have the money or the time to paint the hallway but he didn't know I'd already bought the paint and I just didn't have the mental energy to give anyone an answer to anything so I decided it would make the most sense to leave your message unread so I'd remember to go back and reply later except it got buried by other messages I also didn't read and even though I've only had this phone for two months I somehow have thirty-three unread texts and I just get completely overwhelmed every time I look at my home screen and now it's been like five weeks since you texted and I've thought about writing you back a million times but I was trying to come up with something more original than "so sorry for the late reply!" because that's what I always say and when I finally decided I was just going to pretend I missed your text altogether and come in with the classic but impenetrable "oh shit I missed this!" I realized you probably already found the answer elsewhere and that replying at this point would only result in yet another reply from you and it just seemed like the responsible thing to do was to delete your message so it would stop haunting me and now you're probably mad at me.

Street Drugs

In fifth grade, I won the DARE essay contest. This was back when kids wrote by hand on paper, so I'm sad to say there's no digital trail. And though I can't quite recall the particulars of my award-winning prose for Drug Abuse Resistance Education, I do remember being a very uptight and self-righteous ten-year-old who vowed to do everything in my power to keep my friends and family off of "dope" for the rest of my time on earth. The indoctrination had turned me into a precocious foot soldier in the war on drugs.

A drug, by the way, is "any substance that affects the way your mind and body work"—which I know because that same year, I also won the DARE vocabulary contest. My prize was a giant stuffed teddy bear. Yes, I would be so much cooler if I'd later used Big Stuffy to smuggle cocaine across an international border, but alas, that's not where this story is going.

While I was busy memorizing jargon for my Narc Cadet Toolkit and penning opinion pieces only Carrie Nation could love, I failed to notice that nearly everyone around me was high on what was then referred to as "crystal meth." It was a truly spectacular case of "out of sight, out of mind" considering I grew up in the literal Methamphetamine Capital of America—an honor bestowed upon my hometown of Independence, Missouri, by *Rolling Stone* magazine in the nineties.

My so-called innocence didn't last. By the time I was twelve or thirteen, I was well aware meth was a local problem. It just wasn't a problem I associated with the humans I saw out in the real world. How I failed to make the connection between my methy low-income suburb of Kansas City and its residents is beyond me. I don't know who I thought was doing enough meth to earn us such notoriety, but until I was long gone from Independence, I lived under the assumption that most people I saw around town were skinny and had bad teeth because they were poor. (We were poor, too, but my dad's cousin was a dentist, so we were lucky to get discounted dental care.) I didn't even connect the dots when I got into yelling matches with my little sister's best friend's mom—a woman whose house had a faint but constant chemical smell I knew well but always assumed was a gas leak. I have no recollection of what this lady and I argued about, but I guarantee I wasn't spewing DARE bullshit at her. Even though she was rail thin, completely toothless, and screaming at teenagers, I *still* didn't think to myself, *Hold the phone, Emily. This lady is likely high on meth right now. You should tell Mom so Jo won't have any more playdates IN A FUCKING METH HOUSE.*

Okay, so I was a little naive. But I wasn't a total Pollyanna; I was bitching out tweakers, after all.

I was also developing a taste for the sauce. And by "the sauce," I mean alcohol, in case you're not an old man and didn't catch that drift.

My very first sip of booze was the sweet, sweet (oh, so very sweet) essence of a Bartles & Jaymes wine cooler. It was pink. I was fourteen. And I liked it because it did exactly what my fifth-grade DARE officer—a fifty-something woman with very blonde "closer to Jesus" hair and a tanning salon punch card—promised it would: it changed the way my mind and body worked, but most notably, my mind. Halfway through one bottle, I found it so much easier to talk to people. And by "people," I mostly mean boys, in case you didn't catch that drift, either.

Though my pink malt beverage fit the definition of a "drug"—the definition that had been burned into my brain for eternity, apparently—was it *really* a drug? It was barely wine. And as far as I knew, there was no war on wine.

Besides, if it were really so bad, it wouldn't have been sold at a gas station. Just like my daily cappuccino (which was probably 50 percent high-fructose corn syrup) and my beloved NoDoz.

NoDoz is 200 milligrams of pure caffeine in pill form. And for the last two years of high school, it was my dirty little secret. I'm not saying there was anything dirty about NoDoz—one pill was basically the equivalent of two cups of coffee—but after that iconic *Saved by the Bell* episode in which Jessie Spano becomes addicted to caffeine pills ("I'm so excited! I'm so . . . I'm so . . . *scared*!"), it just felt like something I should keep to myself. Unlike Jessie, I wasn't headed toward a breakdown right before my big commercial debut, and I didn't even have the jitters.

Still, that my dopamine-deficient brain managed to avoid meth while growing up in the Meth Capital of the World *kinda* makes me a DARE success story. In fact, it might have been my reputation as a revered DARE essayist that saved me, because I somehow managed to reside in the heart of meth country and was never once offered the stuff. And that's a very good thing because now that I think about it, I probably would have *loved* meth. At least until it ruined my teeth. And then my life.

Chemically, meth and stimulants (the most commonly prescribed drugs for ADHD) aren't all that different. Both contain amphetamines, which help to increase dopamine levels in the brain. There's even a prescription version of methamphetamine that's sold under the brand name Desoxyn. I don't know anyone who's ever been on it—it's very rarely prescribed these days—but when ADHD naysayers claim that "Adderall is just meth in pill form," Desoxyn is what they're talking about, whether they know it or not. But they've got it backward. Though methamphetamine predates the FDA by thirteen years, street meth is a horrible, dangerous bootleg Desoxyn.

I do sometimes wonder if my complete avoidance of "the bad stuff" was less about me and my early works on substance abuse, and more about my age. Because, given where I grew up, it's entirely possible that my DARE officer had worked so tirelessly to drill into my head the dangers of drugs because I was in the class of 2000.

Since kindergarten, teachers, principals, and other adults brought in to teach Very Important Life Lessons often told my classmates and me how special we were based on the mere fact that we would graduate at the turn of the millennium (most of us, anyway). And if any class was going to make it through high school in Independence, Missouri, without becoming addicted to meth, it was going to be mine. I didn't really see the big deal—wouldn't it be cooler to be *born* in the year 2000?—but that year CBS News published a book about us called *The Class of 2000: A Definitive Study of the New Generation*, so maybe people thought we were going to change the world or something. (So sorry to disappoint.) But the ego stroking may have worked, because of all the sad stories I've heard about people from my high school lost—in one way or another—to meth, not a single one was from my class. Every kid who grew up in the eighties and nineties equated a brain on drugs with a fried egg, but it seems my class was uniquely terrified of that particular fate.

The summer after graduation, I finally made my escape to Brooklyn—where I didn't even need an ID to buy the good Sudafed! I'd left the land of meth and gas station cappuccinos and, as I would quickly learn, landed in the land of no NoDoz. It surely existed somewhere in the city, but not at any of the bodegas or cramped grocery stores I frequented.

Yet I don't remember being too upset about it. For about a year, that new-to-New-York energy was the only stimulant I needed. Okay, not the *only* one. I was still drinking lots of coffee—New York City style, of course ("Cream and two sugars, please!"). Whenever the new wore off, I moved. Not out of the city, just to a more interesting part of it. Over the course of the decade I lived in New York City, I lived in nine different apartments in eight different neighborhoods, including Midwood, Brooklyn (where I stood out like a platinum blonde sore thumb among the Orthodox Jews), both the East and West Villages, and Brighton Beach—an extremely Russian neighborhood right next to Coney Island. I had a few apartments in cool

Brooklyn neighborhoods like Boerum Hill and Greenpoint, too, but both got cooler after I left.

And then, every time I'd feel the ennui start to creep back in, I'd simply change my job, my apartment, my hair color, my major, my dating website of choice (we didn't have apps back then). At least twice, I came really close to adopting a dog. It's a damn good thing I never quite had enough money to do it.

As I became somewhat more settled—with a lease, a boy-friend, a cat—I got restless. I wasn't exactly depressed, but I wasn't motivated to do anything, either. I remember joking to a friend that I wish they made Viagra for your brain. "So I can get it up for work, you know?"

Then, one night at a loft party in Bushwick, a ridiculously handsome and painfully hip guy handed me a different little blue pill.

"Um, what is this?" I asked, as if I wasn't already preparing to swallow it. I was craving an adventure.

"It's like Ritalin, the stuff kids with ADD take," he said, kind of seductively nodding at me, but leading with his chin.

I washed down my very first Adderall with a swig of what-ever cheap beer we were drinking. An hour later, I headed back to my apartment to finish an article I'd been trying to write for a week. The fog that had been preventing my brain from putting words on the page had lifted. It was like someone had scooped all the distractions right out of my head and all I had to do was sit down and let the prose come out. It was the same rush of inspiration and motivation that before had only sur-faced with new ideas and projects far more exciting than an eight-hundred-word piece of service journalism. It was like . . . Viagra? But for work?

After I knocked out the story, I considered washing dishes, but I didn't want to wake my roommate, so I cleaned my room instead. It felt so good to crawl into bed in a tidy space, having turned in my damn story to boot.

Is this *what being an adult feels like?* I wondered.

When I woke up, I thought a lot about that Adderall. I looked forward to trying it again someday, but it didn't cross my mind to seek it out. After all, I wasn't "the kind of person who did drugs." And I certainly wasn't the kind of person who *bought* drugs, definitely not illicit rich-kid drugs like coke, heroin, or, um, children's ADD meds?

The next time someone offered me Adderall at a party, I decided to pocket it for a Monday. After that, I didn't touch the stuff for a few years—not until I had a big cookbook project to finish. I asked a writer friend to help me get a few pills. "Just to help me be done with this damn book," I told him (and myself).

After nearly a decade in New York, I was itching for something new, and a big, cheap apartment lured me back to Kansas City (but *not* Independence) at the beginning of 2009. I loved having a new-old place all to myself, a new city to acclimate to, and the feeling that anything could happen. But unlike New York, which always felt so alive, Kansas City felt like a sleepy town and more so after dark. Everyone drove everywhere. There was no wandering into a bar or a store for an adventure. Hopping on a bus just to see where it would take me was a dangerous "plan" because so many of the buses stopped running after

8:00 p.m.—and this was long before the days Uber and Lyft would allow me to request a ride if I got stranded somewhere.

After I filled all the rooms of my cavernous prewar flat with thrifted furniture, then painted each room (including the kitchen cabinets) different shades of blue and green, I was bored again. So once again, I turned to my party drug of choice: alcohol. But my social drinking quickly turned into the kind of drinking that made me cringe the next morning, which was boring in its own weird way. Desperate for a big change, I decided I would quit drinking for six months, or maybe a year, and train for a half marathon while raising money for cancer research. What I didn't tell anyone was that I was also quitting to convince myself, more than anyone else, that I *could*.

I was excited to be sober for a while—and to toss my hangover corn, a bag of frozen corn I kept in the freezer for exactly one purpose. Though I missed the social lubricant of alcohol, I didn't *need* it, especially because, like Forrest Gump before me, *I was running!* I mean, it was really more of a slow jog, but I had a plan, and a fundraising goal, and fancy new running shoes. I had also developed a taste for frosted animal crackers, the kind with sprinkles, and Diet Coke.

A few months into my sober period, I could jog a few miles straight without feeling like I was going to die. By then, I was also confident that I wasn't an alcoholic, even if I had a bit of a drinking problem. Was it possible that I'd (maybe) just replaced booze with "running" and, um, animal crackers and Diet Coke? Sure. But that didn't seem like the worst thing in the world.

This was right around the time I met Kyle. I left our first date—during which we drank club soda and talked for hours on end—thinking *I might marry this guy*, and things progressed quickly. Unlike nearly every other relationship I'd had, it wasn't stressful, but it was still thrilling because everything felt new and every milestone came with a rush of new-love dopamine. Two months into dating, we met each other's families, and a month after that, he moved into my apartment because his lease was up and we were always at each other's places anyway. Six months into my break from drinking, I reintroduced alcohol in a much more grown-up way—a couple of cocktails here, a shared bottle of wine there—and Kyle and I started to plan the rest of our lives together.

A few months before our wedding, a coworker (I was doing communications for a coffee roaster at this time) who'd recently lost a ton of weight let me in on her secret: she'd been taking diet pills.

"But not the shady kind," she half-whispered. "They're prescription—from a doctor."

A week later, I was sitting in his waiting room, eager for my first thirty-day supply of phentermine—an M.D.-prescribed "amphetamine substitute" that promised to help me lose a few pounds before I had to squeeze into a wedding dress. (Never mind that I was having the dress custom made.) And let me tell you: these pills were magic. I quickly dropped ten pounds, which was great, but more than that, they helped me focus on my work, keep up with dishes, and maintain conversations I didn't want to have for longer than five minutes. They also turned me into a monster; imagine if The Hulk and Bridezilla had a baby who was a thirty-year-old woman. Kyle threatened to call off our wedding if I didn't stop taking them.

So, I stopped. And my brain fogged up again. I tried to counteract the murkiness with exercise, low-carb diets, and high-protein snacks. And it worked, a little, but it just wasn't the same. My brain wandered when it should have been working, and I snacked incessantly. Now I realize I was doing whatever I could to give myself a much-needed dopamine boost, but back then I beat myself up for not having any willpower while stuffing more Cool Ranch Doritos in my face. It was an awful feeling and I probably wallowed in it longer than I should have. Desperate to feel better, I prepaid for six weeks of fitness classes before the wedding and threw myself into exercise. But like everything else I'd attempted in my life, it wasn't sustainable.

Not long after Kyle and I were married, I felt like I was drowning at work (a different job, this time working as a cookbook publicist), so I went back to the doctor, just to get a one-month supply of the totally shady diet pills. Previously, the sleep deprivation hadn't caught up with me until a few weeks into the first bottle, so I figured I could probably take them for a month without Kyle noticing. When I felt myself filling with rage a week or so in, I tried splitting the pills in half. Rationing them still gave me at least five or six hours of focus every day, without sacrificing sleep, or a significant amount of sustenance. It also meant I had three more weeks' worth of pills.

I covertly visited the shady doctor for "just one more thirty-day supply" of his shady pills a couple more times before I started trying to get pregnant, at which point I immediately stopped taking anything other than an organic prenatal vitamin. But after experiencing a clear brain for extended periods of time, the return of the mental fog was almost unbearable.

Once again, I started eating. Anything, everything, all the time. The act of putting food in my face, of chewing, of swallowing, it all felt good—until I stopped, so then I'd eat some more. Predictably, I gained weight, but more troubling was that, hungry or not, I just couldn't seem to stop eating. I decided to try Overeaters Anonymous. It's based on AA and, although I didn't love the religious aspect, I could relate to the other women's stories of uncontrollable eating. What I couldn't get over, though, was the overarching theme of coming out of the program "a different person" than the one who first walked through the door.

"But I don't want to be a different person," I repeatedly told my sponsor. "I just want to be a version of me who doesn't eat an entire jar of peanut butter in two days."

A positive pregnancy test was a great excuse for me to slip out of OA. The entire first trimester felt like an extended hangover, and I knew that if I tried to stick to any sort of regimented diet or eating plan while growing an entire human inside me, I'd fail and feel even worse. So I hit the peanut butter—hard—and made clear to everyone that I was not going to be one of those people who gave up my coffee while pregnant or breastfeeding.

Fifteen months after Teddy was born, I got my hands on my first postpartum Adderall. Kyle and I had tickets to a Radiohead show and we were meeting friends for dinner and drinks beforehand. I was exhausted and filled with social anxiety, so I asked a coworker (another different job this time) if he could spare one pill. I'd already decided I was done with nursing and figured that in addition to helping me function, the Adderall could be the reason I finally fully weaned Teddy. The night was fun and easy, and I didn't fall asleep in my seat during the show. A win!

The next day, though, I found myself wishing I'd saved the little blue pill, or at least half of it, for actual work. So I texted yet another friend to ask him if I could buy some of his pills. (And, yes, in case you haven't noticed, back then, everyone I knew who had been officially diagnosed with ADHD was a man.)

"I'm happy to share a few, but I only have so many and I do need them," he wrote back. "Let me give you the name of this guy I know."

And that, dear reader, is how I became a person who buys drugs—a troubled protagonist in my very own DARE PSA. For about six months, I met this guy in a parking garage and bought as much Adderall as he'd sell me at ten bucks a pop. It was never enough for me to take a pill (or even half a pill) every day, so I'd ration it for my biggest projects and most stressful deadlines, often cutting it into halves or sometimes quarters. This went on until the overwhelm of trying to hold everything together—marriage, motherhood, work, a house—finally backed me into the corner of self-awareness.

Now I know that because of my ADHD, my brain has issues receiving the neurotransmitter dopamine, the body's feel-good chemical that helps regulate emotion. Without some sort of dopamine trigger, I often get lethargic and have a hard time focusing on my day-to-day life. It's one of the reasons many people with ADHD are misdiagnosed with bipolar disorder; a rush of inspiration followed by a late-night painting project or online shopping spree can easily be confused with a manic episode. And it's why I would so quickly and easily get bored with jobs, apartments, hairstyles, and relationships. It also helps explain why many people with ADHD are prone to drug and alcohol abuse—those substances provide dopamine, too—and why treating an addiction that might not really be an addiction often fails.

I'm grateful to finally have a diagnosis and medication that works—though it's not exactly easy to get it, even now. Vyvanse is such a controlled substance that I have to see my psychiatrist every three months and I can't request a refill online. Instead, I must sit through three minutes of voice prompts to speak to a real, live human. And every time I go to pick up my perfectly legal, medically necessary, doctor-prescribed stimulants, I feel like everyone is watching me.

Does the pharmacist think I'm one of those rich kids who started taking ADHD meds when I was sixteen to gain some sort of academic edge? Do the techs see me as a mom popping pills for recreation instead of a whole person who needs a prescription for a brain that doesn't process dopamine the same way most people's brains do? They probably don't even know I have kids, but somehow they still classify me as a bad mom; I'm sure of it. And what about the people in line behind me? When the pharmacist asks me what medication I'm picking up and I say "the Vyvanse," what are those strangers thinking about me? I know I shouldn't care, but I do.

Maybe all those trolls and quacks who claim "ADHD isn't real" got inside my head and stayed in there somewhere, just to remind me that I really am lazy and messy and could do a better job of getting places on time if I just tried a little harder.

Maybe I should start exercising more. Maybe I self-medicated for too long.

Sometimes (okay, a lot of the time) I think that texting some dude and meeting him in a parking garage was so much easier than keeping up with my prescription. But instead of reaching out to him again, I switched to a CVS with a drive-through pharmacy.

Did You Try This First?

CrossFit.

Waking up at 4:30 a.m. six days a week to fit in three quick hours of high-intensity cardio. (Before CrossFit, of course.)

Any exercise.

An exorcism.

Essential oils.

Certified therapeutic grade™ essential oils.

Making your bed. It sets the tone for your whole day, you know.

Cutting back on caffeine.

Quadrupling your caffeine intake.

Adding some essential oils to your coffee.

Adding some *certified therapeutic grade*™ essential oils to your coffee.

Quitting coffee completely and just drinking straight peppermint oil every morning.

Quitting coffee completely and just drinking *certified therapeutic grade*™ straight peppermint oil every morning.

Vitamin injections.

Hormone injections.

Caffeine injections.

Essential oil injections.

Certified therapeutic grade™ essential oil injections.

Colonic irrigation.

Trying harder to be on time.

Apple cider vinegar gummies.

Drinking straight apple cider vinegar. The one with the mother.

Soaking your whole body in a bath of apple cider vinegar warmed to exactly 103.6°F for two hours every night.

Eliminating Blue Dye No. 1 from your diet.

Eating more protein.

The Caveman Diet.

The Paleo Diet.

The Atkins Diet.

The South Beach Diet.

The Cabbage Soup Diet.

A shake for breakfast, a shake for lunch, and a sensible dinner.

Adopting a gluten-free, sugar-free, texture-free diet.

Replacing all of your meals with green juice and supplements.

Intermittent fasting.

Eating more often.

Eating one unsalted cashew every fifteen minutes and
  nothing else.

Eating activated charcoal more often.

Eating that Kingsford flavored charcoal. Maybe the
  Basil Sage Thyme?

Meditating.

No, but like, *really* meditating.

Losing ten pounds.

Trying harder to get out of bed in the morning.

Bullet journaling.

Bullet journaling but with really cute gel pens.

Drinking your own urine. (You can add some La
  Croix to dilute it if you want.)

Drinking your own urine, diluted with La Croix
  and flavored with *certified therapeutic grade*™
  essential oil.

Dianetics.

Chicken soup.

Chicken Soup for the Soul.

Soul Cycle.

Doing Molly.

Being poly.

Just working ahead so you're never behind.

Steaming your vagina.

Vitamin D supplements.

Getting more sun.

Sunning your vagina.

Finding Jesus.

Finding Jesus and then losing him and then finding
   him again but ultimately losing him because you
   lose everything.
Sleeping more.
Going to bed earlier.
Going to bed ever.
Getting a whole new bed so you'll be excited about
   going to bed.
Just forcing yourself to go to bed at a decent hour.
Hot yoga.
Hot Pockets.
Applying yourself.
Applying leeches to yourself.
A sensory deprivation tank.
An exotic fish tank, for meditation, duh.
Reading a Malcolm Gladwell book.
Believing in yourself.
Putting your mind to it, going for it, getting down,
   and breaking a sweat.
Watching your weight. Not necessarily doing
   anything about it. Just obsessively *watching* it.
Watching Dr. Oz, but just reruns since he's a
   politician now.
Watching *The Wizard of Oz*.
Watching *Return to Oz*.
Making your own perfume out of mood-boosting
   essential oils.
Making your own perfume out of *certified therapeutic
   grade*™ mood-boosting essential oils.

Building a time machine and traveling back to
   1982 to show your mom all the new "research" on
   vaccines.
A fecal transplant.
Cloning yourself.
Cloning yourself and feeding the clone only green
   juice and supplements.
Cloning yourself and feeding the clone only green
   juice and supplements, then getting a fecal
   transplant from your much-healthier clone.
Trying harder. But using essential oils while you do it.
   Just make sure they're *certified therapeutic grade*™.

A Breakup Story

"You make casseroles and you sing bad karaoke. And you're just, like, really intense."

Those were the reasons my first serious boyfriend, Rich, gave after telling me he didn't see us having a future together. Right after we'd had sex. Two days before Valentine's Day.

If you've ever been called "intense," you know that ten times out of ten, it's meant as an insult. And if you have ADHD, you know the intensity is unavoidable when you get excited about something new.

Unfortunately, I didn't know any of this when I met Rich—who sold himself as "an artist and DJ"—in my early twenties at a meetup for young political activists that was really more of an excuse to drink free beer with like-minded people. In fact, I thought I'd played the whole relationship thing *extremely cool* and regularly told him, "If at any point you no longer see us having a future together, I want you to tell me."

I guess I was even intense about trying to be cool.

Of course, I didn't believe he'd actually ever come to that conclusion and I couldn't envision any scenario that didn't involve us splitting the astronomical rent on the top floor (or maybe the garden apartment) of a Brooklyn brownstone, not unlike the apartment he lived in but with much better decor and without an antisocial roommate fifteen years his senior. There'd be babies someday, too, but not before years of nonstop Scrabble played at the handmade coffee table while sitting on a fancy imported rug that was much more expensive than it looked.

A few hours before Rich dropped the breakup bomb, he cooked dinner while I installed his very first wireless network. I named it after what I'd decided was our song, "Islands in the Stream," the Kenny Rogers and Dolly Parton duet we had performed *together* at karaoke on more than one occasion. After I washed the dinner dishes, I walked up to him, lovingly patted his big belly, gave him a kiss, and said, "I love that I fix things and that you cook." He rolled his bloodshot eyes and ran his hand through his greasy brown hair. Apparently, he didn't appreciate this unofficial arrangement as much as I did. But as far as I was concerned, I was living out my progressive East Coast couple fantasy with a stay-at-home boyfriend who made all our meals.

Rich was five years older than me and had been raised by academics in the Bay Area. He wanted to be a writer and fancied himself a food snob. Because his parents paid his rent, he could laze around the farmers' market on a random Tuesday, then get high and spend three hours making dinner. I grew up in subsidized housing in Missouri and for the last few years had been hosting an annual casserole cook-off for Midwestern transplants in Williamsburg. I was taking night classes (and one very primitive online course) in my fifth year of undergrad at the New School, working a short-lived full-time job in non-profit communications, and trying to get freelance writing assignments on the side. Most months, I struggled to make my half of the rent on the crusty Greenpoint apartment I'd more or less left to my roommate in favor of Rich's much roomier place (where there was always fancy cheese in the fridge).

I honestly thought he would ask me to move in soon, but I guess I'd been too busy daydreaming about a living room makeover to notice any warning signs.

What did he mean he couldn't see us having a future together? Okay, I might have been a little intense, but I was also kind of a catch. I had a job. I only beat him at Scrabble, like, 53 percent of the time. I was quite good (if, yes, intense) at a wide range of karaoke hits. And people fucking loved my casserole parties, thank you very much. Plus, I often worried everyone secretly hated me and I was fairly certain his friends and family all loved me. Most notable, perhaps, is that after nearly two years, we were still having sex daily, sometimes twice a day. (Though, even when he was high, there were some things he refused to eat.)

"*You're* breaking up with *me*?" I asked him, as tears started to trickle down the red blotches I could feel lighting up my face and neck. "Why?"

He looked down at his limp dick and that's when he said it.

"You make casseroles and you sing bad karaoke."

(After eighteen months, that was all he could come up with?!)

"And you're just, like, really intense."

(Right. There was also that.)

I couldn't breathe. I had to poop. Or vomit. Maybe both at the same time. My head was spinning from the shock and I decided I needed to punish him; it was the only way to deal with what I was feeling.

Intense?! I thought. *I'll fucking show him intense.*

This silent proclamation was as practical as it was emotional. February in New York City is brutal and the temperature had been hovering around five degrees Fahrenheit for days. He was stuck with me. At least for the night.

Rich was never any good at dealing with me when I cried, so I buried myself in his bed, nuzzled my swollen, snot-covered face into his pillow, and stayed up weeping and shivering next to him until the physical and emotional exhaustion took over. I fell into a half sleep and he sneaked into the living room to smoke a joint—which was enough to rouse me from my nap, so I wandered into the living room after him.

My nose was still runny and for a second, I forgot I was supposed to be mad.

"Are you . . . [sniff, sniff] *serious?*"

He was.

How could this be happening to me? We were in love. At least that's what I thought the endless stream of cutsey couple selfies I posted relentlessly to Flickr indicated. For our first Valentine's Day together, he'd made me a snickerdoodle with Red Hots (my favorite candy) baked into a heart shape and a "terms of endearment" dinner—lamb chops, baby vegetables, and sweet peas. He'd seen it on Rachael Ray's *30 Minute Meals.* It was the first time anyone had done anything for me on Valentine's Day since my boyfriend in the tenth grade bought a single red rose off of his friend Rodney when he got to school because he'd forgotten it was Valentine's Day. (It should be noted that Rodney got his roses at a gas station. It should also be noted that red roses are among my least favorite flowers.)

Anyway, I crawled back into his bed and *tried* to cry myself to sleep.

Rich passed out on the couch and I stayed in his bed alone, curled into a ball, awake and devastated until the sun came up. I took a shower and got dressed, all the while imagining he'd come to tell me he'd made the biggest mistake of his life. I'd never brushed my teeth with such intensity and feeling, waiting for the most important moment of my life to happen. The soundtrack to my heartbreak (Lisa Loeb, Toni Braxton, Boyz II Men, to name a few) played in my head as I watched myself move the brush up and down and up and down. I didn't want to stop until he came up behind me and told me that he had been confused and lost but that the idea of me going away for good was simply too much for him to handle. I'd melt into his arms and he'd lead me to the bed and finally go dow—

But he never showed up in the mirror. So I stopped brushing my teeth when my gums began to bleed. Or once I noticed they were bleeding.

I decided I would go to work, but as I started to walk out his door and he didn't stop me I burst into tears again. It felt like the last time I would ever leave his apartment. I pulled myself together long enough to call in sick (my nose full of snot really worked in my favor) and packed as many things as I could carry with me. I tried to be really dramatic about it all, hastily shoving my blow dryer, my retainer, and my dirty underwear in the same plastic Duane Reade bag. But one can only be so dramatic when a retainer is involved. Still, I wanted him to see how much I hurt, and I wanted that to hurt him. If it did hurt him, he didn't let it show.

I must have looked really pathetic on my long, cold walk to the subway because a man on his bike pulled up next to me and stopped.

"You okay, lady?" he shouted in a thick New York City accent and almost got hit by a bus.

At least I haven't been hit by a bus, I thought and was comforted by that idea, until I sat down on the train and quickly realized that I'd rather have been hit by a bus. Again, I burst into tears and snot (I still don't understand how a not-sick person produces so much snot!) and sniffled my way through all nine stops from Gowanus to Greenpoint.

I went back to my stale apartment and tried to eat. I couldn't. It was the first time in my life—save for the few times I was really sick—that I couldn't manage to swallow any food. I tried to sleep, too. But I was awake for thirty-six hours before a red wine and cannabis cocktail finally did the trick.

As soon as I started to fall asleep the phone rang. It was him . . . he maybe, sort of, might have made the wrong decision, but he wasn't sure. But he wanted to tell me that he wasn't sure. In the state I was in, that was enough for me to close my eyes for a few hours.

As soon as I woke up, I called him.

In our usual fashion, I tried to fix things and insisted he cook me Valentine's Day dinner the following night. I don't remember what we ate, and we may or may not have slept together; my memory from that night is hazy, at best. But my stomach was full, we smoked a bowl, and I fell asleep in his bed. It was the first time I'd really slept in days.

The next morning, while he played it cool on his ugly couch, I moved the rest of my stuff out of his apartment. As I packed (much less dramatically this time), I thought to myself, *I hope he never figures out how to change the name of his wireless network.* It was the closest I could get to haunting his ass.

Recently, my sister and I were drinking wine on my much-more-stylish couch in Kansas City and reminiscing about my time in New York. Rich came up and she looked him up on Facebook.

"He got married," she said. "Oh! *Today!*"

"Oh, good for him," I said. And I meant it. It felt good to not feel a thing. But I'd be lying if I didn't wonder how long it took him to rename his Wi-Fi network.

Self-Assessment

1. How often do you have trouble wrapping up the final details of a project, once the challenging parts have been done?

Hmm. How broke am I in this scenario? I mean, sometimes, even when I'm broke, I'm not great about sending invoices. But I've tried to be a lot better about paperwork in the last few years. It really just made me realize how much I need an assistant. Though I think I'd take a housekeeper before an assistant. Is there someone who would do both? Or do life managers exist? Because I need one of those. Especially if they'll pay my bills for me—with my own money, of course! Not that I have much, though I don't know because I haven't looked at my bank account in a while. Which is exactly why I need someone to manage my finances for me. But you probably mean the project itself and not the stuff that comes after, right? Before you even get to the invoicing? Yeah, I guess I do have trouble with that. I started my friend Rachel's website about three years ago and there are just some little things I have to do to finish it. Every day when I see "JUST FUCKING FINISH RACHEL'S WEB-SITE!!!" on my to-do list my stomach drops. I'm sure I could get the whole thing done in about an hour, but for some reason, I can't. Oh, and then there are my taxes. . . .

2. How often do you have difficulty getting things in order when you have to do a task that requires organization?

Oh! That is *not* a problem. I can spend hours organizing things. Sometimes, before I have to start a big project, I'll rename all the files for it so they have the same exact naming convention. It doesn't affect the final outcome, but it looks so nice and usually inspires me to clean up all the other files on my hard drive. I also like to organize my kids' Legos by color. It's so calming, like meditation—or what I think meditation would be like but I don't really know because I can't meditate. I just like sorting and organizing things. You wouldn't know it by looking at my house, which is really messy and unorganized at the moment (it looks like someone threw up Legos all over the playroom right now), but when I do get inspired to organize, there's no stopping me. I have this little Bluetooth label maker I bought before Teddy started kindergarten and I thought I was just going to label a few things, but then I ended up labeling *everything*. Like, every single crayon, colored pencil, and marker. It was very satisfying! So now, when I organize things in the house, I put labels on the drawers and shelves and containers to help me *stay* organized. It sometimes works?

When I do finally sit down to send everything to my tax guy—months after he filed yet another extension on my behalf—I will hand him the most organized documents he'll see all year. Except I won't literally hand them to him because it's not 1987. I'll upload everything to his client portal or whatever. I feel like I need to make that clear because I don't want you to picture me, like, handing a dude in a suit a manila folder full of coffee-stained tax documents, because that's not a thing I'd do (though I do have boxes and envelopes full of tattered receipts stashed all over the damn place just in case I ever get audited). But while we're talking about online portals, can we talk about how Dropbox is a total racket? Because it is. Ask me about it later, though. Because if I get started on that, we'll never get through this. . . . But seriously, did you realize they charge the person sharing the file AND the person viewing the file? And if you run out of space, even with files that aren't yours, they make you pay to access them??? Total. Fucking. Racket. I honestly can't believe anyone still uses it. You don't use Dropbox, do you? If so, you should find something else. Seriously. Really, though, if you're still using Dropbox you need to change to Google Docs or something.

3. How often do you have problems remembering appointments or obligations?

Right now I have this pretty under control. Well, as long as I enter events into my calendar correctly, which I don't always do. But when everything is entered with the right date and time, I'm usually good because I figured out a way to get Google to send me an email every morning with my agenda for the day. Unfortunately, seeing a note about a meeting in the morning doesn't always translate to remembering it six hours later, so everything that gets added to my calendar also has three default notifications. One comes via email and two are pop-ups that go to my phone, computer, other computer, iPad, and Apple Watch. That watch has been life-changing, by the way. I set it up so the face will show me what my next appointment is so it's always right there on my wrist. Isn't that amazing?! I can also use my watch to find my phone, which I lose about seven times a day. The other morning I was running around looking for it and it was in my hand! I hadn't had my coffee yet and my meds hadn't kicked in, but still!

4. When you have a task that requires a lot of thought, how often do you avoid or delay getting started?

Just making a note here so I remember to come back to this one.

5. How often do you fidget or squirm with your hands or feet when you have to sit down for a long time?

Maybe a better question is: Are you worried about getting a blood clot from sitting for extended periods of time? Because I am. I went down a rabbit hole reading about deep vein thrombosis the other night and that's some scary shit. I don't remember how I got there, but the algorithm probably fed me an article about it because I've been looking for the perfect compression socks for weeks and people wear compression socks to prevent blood clots. I recently wore some on a flight and noticed my legs and feet felt so much better than they usually do, so now I think I'm going to be a person who wears compression socks all the time. But I've spent a lot of time looking and mostly there are cute ones with bad reviews and ugly ones with good reviews and I really feel like there's a hole in the market here. Maybe I just need to start my own compression sock brand. It looks like cutecompressionsocks.com is still available to buy, but that's not a very clever name. And it's a little long for a URL. I'll keep thinking on it, but I'll probably go ahead and reserve it now just in case. I already own, like, forty domain names, so what's one more?

6. How often do you feel overly active and compelled to do things, like you were driven by a motor?

I wouldn't call it a motor, I don't think. It's more like, if I decide I need to do something, there's no way it's not going to happen. Does that make sense? There's just this complete physical, mental, and emotional obsession with making it happen. Like, if I don't do it, I'll die of anticipation or something. So I guess, yeah, maybe it is like a motor. So, yeah. A motor. Sure. And now I'm going to have that "motorin'" song stuck in my head, but the title is actually "Sister Christian."

7. How often do you make careless mistakes when you have to work on a boring or difficult project?

Well, I rely on systems to help me avoid mistakes at work. The main one is spell-check. It's not that I can't spell, but sometimes my brain works faster than my fingers can type and it's hard to see the errors in your own work, you know? When I proof-read something I've written, my brain will often just register the word I meant to use and it doesn't always notice the typo. So spell-check is amazing for that, but I do wonder if it's making me a worse speller, or at least lazy. Because sometimes, when a document gets too long and I've opened it too many times, Google seems to give up on underlining my errors and I have to manually run spell-check and I'm sometimes shocked at how many words I've misspelled. Before I knew this was a thing, I turned in a freelance story with a bunch of misspelled words and that was mortifying. I still think about it all the time. All. The. Time.

8. How often do you have difficulty keeping your attention when you are doing boring or repetitive work?

How boring are we talking? If it's *really* boring, I can usually focus for a minute or two before I start opening new tabs. The weird thing is that sometimes I don't even know I'm doing it. I'll be all, *Okay, I'm going to sit down at my computer and finally knock out this story on the proper way to store bread.* Then, all of a sudden, I'm on Amazon looking for a disco ball for my chicken coop or arguing with somebody's racist uncle on a Facebook comment thread.

9. How often do you have difficulty concentrating on what people say to you, even when they are speaking to you directly?

It depends. Are these people trying to talk to me while I'm clearly in the middle of figuring something out? Because Kyle does that all the time and then he gets mad that I'm not giving him my full attention and that's not fair. I've tried to tell him that if he wants to have a serious conversation, he needs to give me a little bit of notice—some time to get into the right mindset for it, you know? Maybe put it on my calendar. But definitely send me an invite so I don't enter it incorrectly. Of course, seeing an impending conversation on my agenda will fill me with anxiety, but it's better than interrupting me when I'm hyperfocused . . . I think?

10. How often do you misplace or have difficulty finding things at home or at work?

This is less of a problem than it used to be because now I have systems. And Apple AirTags. I have one on my keychain, in my purse, in my kids' bags. I love that my phone and watch will buzz me if I leave something behind. Another trick is buying items in multiples. For example, there's this amazing microfiber cloth I use to clean my glasses and I would be so angry if I couldn't find it, so I have one in my purse, one in my nightstand, one on my desk, one in the bathroom, one in the car, and one on a hook in my little closet/dressing room. Now there's always one wherever I happen to be and I never have to move them—which means I'll never lose them. Brilliant, if I do say so myself.

11. How often are you distracted by activity or noise around you?

Sometimes the sound of the air conditioner is so distracting that I have to turn it off to write, but I also can't fall asleep without a fan or the TV on. What's up with that?

12. How often do you leave your seat in meetings or other situations in which you are expected to remain seated?

Need I remind you about the risk of deep vein thrombosis from sitting too much? Also, this feels like a trick question because I drink a lot of coffee and I have a small bladder. But I guess if I'm not actively engaged in a meeting I tend to get sleepy and getting up and moving around helps me refocus my brain. Other times, I'll be really into a project and look at the clock and realize I've been sitting at my desk for six hours. And that I'm hungry. And have to pee.

13. How often do you feel restless or fidgety?

See above.

14. How often do you have difficulty unwinding and relaxing when you have time to yourself?

This feels like another trick question because I never have time to myself. But the next time I do, I'm going to deep clean the fridge. And maybe the freezer, too! Oh, and I need to dye my hair. And I should probably also tackle some of that laundry in the basement. When I do that, I hope I'll finally be inspired to organize my tool corner, too. It was super organized when I set it up (seriously, it looked like a hardware store) and now it's just a heap of boxes and bowls full of tools and sandpaper and paint and random hardware and probably lots of spiders.

15. How often do you find yourself talking too much when you are in social situations?

Would you ask a man this question? Pass. My hand is getting crampy.

16. When you're in a conversation, how often do you find yourself finishing the sentences of the people you are talking to, before they can finish them themselves?

Okay, this is definitely one of my bad habits. But sometimes people just take SO LONG to finish a sentence and, hey, at least it shows that I'm actively listening, right?

(Are we almost done here? I'd like to be done now.)

17. How often do you have difficulty waiting your turn in situations when turn taking is required?

Ugh. It's not a "difficulty"; I just don't do lines. As far as waiting my turn, I guess I'm usually the first person in line for a buffet. But nobody ever wants to be the first person to go through the buffet line, so I'm actually doing everyone a favor when I go first.

18. How often do you interrupt others when they are busy?

This is definitely a thing I do, but I have a lot of good ideas, and if I don't get a thought out of my head right when I have it, it might go away forever.

Oh, fuck. I was just supposed to rate each of these on a scale from "Never" to "Very Often"? Well, I missed that. Sorry. Yes, now I see that it was written at the top of the page. But I just got excited and started answering the questions. I generally don't bother to read instructions, at least not all the way through, because they're a waste of time. Can you just go back and rank everything for me based my answers here? Because if you make me go back and do it, I'll probably way overthink the difference between "sometimes" and "often" and take a little break to clear my head and it will never get done. But it will continue to live on my to-do list and fill me with shame and anxiety for the next seven months until I finally check it off just to make it go away forever. So, yeah, if there's any way you could just do the ranking for me, that would be great. Thank you!!

What Not to Say to Someone with ADHD

"Yeah, but everybody's a little ADHD."*

No, I Will Not Shut Up About My Abortion

I was still sitting on the toilet as I watched the blue lines slowly intersect.

"Well, it's not quite a plus sign!" I yelled to my boyfriend of three months, Josh, through the bathroom door, trying to ignore that the vertical line—the line that makes a plus sign a plus sign—was most prominent. I was twenty-three and we were at his parents' lake house in the Poconos. It was really more of a compound, complete with a big house, a "little house," and a garden to sustain us. And it was my favorite place on earth, or at least east of the Mississippi. Two months earlier, we'd had a magical (and very drunk) weekend up there and this time we were back for a little R&R. I'd been under the weather for weeks, recovering from a supposedly minor (unrelated) outpatient surgery. The Vicodin I was taking for the pain made me so nauseated that I'd already lost ten pounds.

"You can barely make out that other one," I said, trying to convince both of us that a line wasn't truly a line.

Josh came in to inspect it for himself and we agreed that it kinda sorta looked like a line but definitely probably wasn't a line.

Another wave of nausea came over me and I lowered myself back onto the toilet. I needed an answer and I needed it quickly, so I called the 1-800 number on the box. (This antiquated research method was commonplace in 2005.) I explained to the man on the other end that one line was dark but that the other was so faint I couldn't be sure it was a line at all.

"How dark is the vertical line?" he asked.

"Very dark."

"Then you're very pregnant."

As I hung up the phone, I heard him say, "Congratulations."

How the hell was he allowed to say that?!

I turned to Josh. "Find me the number for Planned Parenthood."

Nobody ever wants to hear about my abortion, but I always want to talk about it. Not because I'm proud of it (I'm not) or ashamed of it (I'm not) or sad about it (I'm not). I talk about my abortion because I know other people are afraid to talk about theirs.

I'm not.

Though I often worry Angry White Man from Twitter will hunt me down and shoot me in front of my children someday (totally normal anxiety, right?), I have enough privilege to feel relatively safe telling my story. So I do.

Three days after I called the number on the back of the EPT box, I sat in the packed waiting room of 26 Bleecker Street (known then as the Margaret Sanger Clinic), waiting for my turn. I was surrounded by women whose lives I couldn't begin to comprehend. Most were Black and Hispanic, and unlike me, nearly all of them were alone. Two stand out: A young Latina mother from Queens who already had four kids and a waspy sixteen-year-old girl who'd taken the train by herself from Long Island. She was going home the same way. Because she couldn't tell anybody in her conservative family about her "condition." And she certainly couldn't tell them she was terminating it. Because people don't talk about their abortions.

I've always been an oversharer and I'm often the loudest person in the room. An even less charming trait is that I sincerely enjoy making people ever-so-slightly uncomfortable with the truth. And my truth is that my story isn't special. It's not tragic, either. I didn't have an abortion because I was trying to save my own life (at least not physically) or because the fetus had some defect that would have led to a miserable existence (at least not that I know of). And I don't expect anyone to change their view on abortion after hearing about my experience. But still, I talk about my abortion.

When I talk about my abortion, I talk about the women I met in the waiting room and that I was one of the lucky ones that day because Josh sat for eight hours in the lobby and took me home in a cab. I recall feeling like I was being herded, a bloated cow shuffled from windowless room to windowless room, waiting for someone to make my body mine again. I laugh a little when I admit that I hate the movie *White Chicks* because that's what the receptionist at Planned Parenthood decided to play on the wall-mounted TV that day (but we can all agree it's a legitimately terrible movie, right?). I talk about coming out of the anesthesia with intense abdominal pain—worse than any cramps I'd ever had—but still feeling relieved that the nausea was finally gone. And I lighten up a little when I admit that I got my appetite back and craved only Kraft Mac & Cheese.

When I talk about my abortion, I go into all the gory detail of bleeding for weeks and weeks and weeks and weeks after. Most of all, I talk about how grateful I am that I had access to safe, legal abortion and a boyfriend who could afford to pay for it because I sure couldn't.

I talk about my abortion because even though I was hyper-focused on *not* getting pregnant, I still slipped up. Before that magical, drunken weekend in the mountains, I'd started back on birth control after a year-long break due to some trouble with insurance paperwork. Apparently, it just hadn't "kicked in" yet. I knew that was a possibility, so as soon as we got back to the city, I called my OB's office and left a message requesting the morning-after pill. Nobody ever called me back, at least not in the two days I frantically answered my phone and checked my voicemail. Then I got busy with work and school and an excruciating surgery where the sun don't shine and once I stopped worrying about it, I just kind of forgot about it completely.

About a month later, I started to experience pregnancy symptoms, but there were other explanations for all of them. My missed period was due to the new contraceptive pills I'd started midcycle and my body was probably still adjusting. The Vicodin was causing the nausea and fatigue. I was getting headaches because I wasn't eating (which also explained the weight loss). Although I considered that I *could* be pregnant, I didn't think I really *was*. I only bought the test to put my mind at ease. And in some ways it did. Though I was surprised by the ominous blue line, it explained why I'd been feeling so awful and it gave me the information I needed to make a plan. Yes, a plan—not a decision. Because there was no decision to be made, no emotional discussion to be had. I was terminating the pregnancy because I wasn't yet ready to be a mother, and wouldn't be for another decade. Especially not in a country that doesn't take care of mothers *or* babies, in a world where a teen mom's most promising path out of poverty is exploiting her life on an MTV reality show.

Because I wasn't ready to be a mother, I should have followed up with my doctor as many times as it took. And someone from her office should have called back after my first message. And I should have continued to check my voicemail in case anyone actually did. And Josh should have worn a condom even though I was on the pill. And Plan B should have been available without a prescription (which did happen the following year). And I should have had easier access to birth control. And insurance shouldn't have been so hard to navigate. But none of those things happened, so I ended up pregnant and then I had an abortion.

I talk about my very unremarkable, legal, safe abortion because I can. Because in my educated, middle-class, liberal world, I can talk about my abortion without having to worry about losing my job, being shunned by my community, getting judged by my partner, or going to jail. And because the people who did have to make heart-wrenching decisions under terrible circumstances shouldn't have to perform their trauma over and over again to make abortion safe and accessible for everyone who needs it.

I talk about my abortion because I can. And because I can, I should. And I'm not going to stop. Well, unless some angry dude from Twitter actually does hunt me down.

Ten Things I Hate About Fruit

If you give me a bag of trail mix, I'll give you back a bag of raisins. Why anyone would put rotten, shriveled grapes in an otherwise fine collection of nuts and chocolate is beyond me. Yet somehow I'm always the weird one just because I don't want to eat little brown scrotums and I can't be in the same room as a ripe banana? I admit my sensory issues mean I'm more easily triggered than most by the repulsive smells and textures of fruit, but I'm not wrong either. Here are the top ten (of many) reasons fruit is the worst.

1. It's dangerous.

Think about how many trees and shrubs grow fruit. I can't give you even a ballpark number and I gave up trying to find one after a few minutes of scrolling bad Google results. But my cursory research tells me there are thousands, if not tens of thousands of fruits just growing all willy-nilly out in the wild for anyone to ingest. Yet humans eat, what? Like, twenty of them? And why don't we eat the rest? BECAUSE THEY COULD

FUCKING KILL US. There's a reason so many stories use poisonous berries as a plot twist: a whole lot of the world's fruit causes hallucinations, seizures, vomiting, and sometimes death. How many early humans had to foam at the mouth and keel over to discover which fruits were okay enough to consume? And don't get me started on the "safe" fruits, either. Apple seeds have cyanide in them, underripe lychee can cause a blood pressure crash, and a friend's kid once got listeria from grocery store peaches. It's all proof that the only safe fruit is no fruit.

2. It's mushy.

There's a real fine line between ripe and rotten. So fine that if you manage to find not-mushy fruit at the market, you only have about twenty-three minutes until things start to go very wrong. And I'm gonna stop there because I'm already dry heaving at the thought of having to chew and swallow an overripe blueberry.

3. It's a sad excuse for dessert.

I've definitely tricked my kids into eating fruit for dessert a time or two. But I am not a gullible child, so don't try to pull that shit on me. A true dessert is made with lots of gluten and refined sugar and preferably a scoop of vanilla bean ice cream. If I show up to a dinner party at your house and you bring me a bowl of berries with whipped cream on top and call it "dessert," you will never see me again.

4. It's full of sugar.

The only reason people get away with serving fruit for dessert is because it's mostly sugar. A single, medium-size banana has

27 grams of carbs—that's nine *more* grams than a beef soft taco from Taco Bell. And you will never convince me a banana is more satisfying than anything on the Taco Bell menu. *Live más*, motherfuckers.

5. It starts to rot the second you slice it.

As soon as you cut into any fruit, it begins to oxidize. Some will immediately turn brown, others will get slimy, and a few will do *both*. You can keep your rotting fruit to yourself, thanks.

6. Fruit salad.

The only thing worse than sliced fruit is sliced fruit coming into contact with *other* sliced fruits. Is one decomposing piece of produce not enough? The next worst thing you could possibly do is toss it in a bowl to rub up against other slimy fruit flesh. Then you just leave it all there to rot together for a few hours until you're ready to serve it to your unsuspecting guests? NO THANK YOU.

7. It's baby food.

I realize fruit isn't just baby food, but lots of baby food *is* just mashed-up fruit. And I will forever associate the general idea of "fruit" with Fruit Dessert,* a 1980s Gerber product made with water ("necessary for preparation"), apricots (from concentrate), pineapple juice (from concentrate), sugar, orange juice (from concentrate), corn starch, and citric acid. My younger sister—a

---

*   Fruit Dessert is not to be confused with a later Gerber product called "Exotic Dessert," which was just another fruity sludge made with the very exotic fruits, banana, pineapple, and mango.

person who loves fruit almost as much as I hate it—ate this putrid purée way past the baby stage. I didn't know exactly what was repulsing me at the time, but it was a smell I now recognize as "rotting fruit salad" (redundant, I know).

8. Edible Arrangements.

Why do these exist? I would rather get an anal fissure than an Edible Arrangement. And by "an anal fissure" I mean "another anal fissure." I know firsthand how painful they are and I stand by this statement.

9. It's unpredictable.

I didn't always hate fruit as much as I do now, at least not *all* fruit. When I was a kid, I'd eat apples with reckless abandon. That is, until I took a bite out of one and revealed a LIVE WORM wiggling right where my mouth had just been. Now I will reluctantly buy apples for my kids (mostly to avoid judgment from other parents), but it takes me forever to pick the perfect Honeycrisp or Gala from the produce pile as I squeeze and closely inspect each one for puncture wounds, soft spots, and *worm holes*. But just because an apple makes it past my rigorous screening one day, doesn't mean it won't be mealy or bug-infested the next. This is why I keep apples in the refrigerator and always, always, always serve them by the slice—never whole.

10. Fruit flies.

There are three things that attract flies as quickly as ripe fruit: garbage, raw meat, and actual shit.

Misdiagnosed

Hysteria is undoubtedly the first mental disorder attributable to women, accurately described in the second millennium BC, and until Freud, considered an exclusively female disease.

— Cecilia Tasca, Mariangela Rapetti,
Mauro Giovanni Carta, and Bianca Fadda,
"Women and Hysteria in the History
of Mental Health"

From the moment the nurse closed the door, I wanted to run out after her and then keep going ("Keep my thirty-dollar co-pay, bitches!") down the five flights of stairs and out to the parking garage where I'd spend ten minutes trying to remember where I parked my midsize SUV in a sea of midsize SUVs.

But I stayed, though the space felt more like an interrogation room than an office. Not that I've ever been in an interrogation room, but it's what I imagine one would look like based on decades of having *Law & Order* on in the background. If I'd been hired to name the paint color on the wall, I'd have called

it "Soft Vom," and the chairs were covered in the type of plas-
ticky vinyl that makes your legs sweat, even through pants. The
worst part, though, was the lack of windows. Was this the kind
of room people tried to jump out of? Is that why there were
two doors, too? So big men in white jackets could walk in and
detain me if I suddenly became hysterical?

It was hard to believe I was on the same floor of the same
building where, just two months earlier, I was cracking jokes
with my OB-GYN while she lubed up a speculum for my first
postpartum Pap smear. This side of the elevator bank ("Psych")
felt like a whole other world—a movie world in which the
antagonist incessantly torments the leading lady until he con-
vinces her and everyone else that she's certifiably crazy so he can
steal her money or her kids or her kidney—or possibly all three.

Just when I started to wonder what was on the other side
of the second door (could I maybe slip out unnoticed?), a
tall, skinny white guy with a beachy tan and dirty blond hair
knocked as he peeked his head in. Then he let himself fully into
the room and extended his hand.

> Difficulties in social interactions in girls with ADHD
> may stem from their choice of action in social situations;
> one study reported that to reach the same social goals,
> 6- to 12-year-old girls with ADHD are more likely to
> respond to hypothetical social vignettes with negative
> and/or aggressive actions than girls without ADHD.
>
> —Patricia O. Quinn and Manisha Madhoo,
> "A Review of Attention-Deficit/Hyperactivity
> Disorder in Women and Girls"

"Emily? Hi. I'm Doctor Woodridge, a psychiatry resident. How are you today?"

He looked to be about my age, if not a few years younger. He also looked like he could have been president of the Young Republicans Club.

"A *resident?*" was all I could muster. Maybe being short with him could make it all end sooner.

His handshake had that repulsive combination of weak and sweaty, which debunked my Young Republican theory since I'm pretty sure a firm grip is part of the conservative swagger.

"Yes, a resident doctor. I am a doctor, and I'm doing a psychiatry rotation. My attending will be in later."

"So, you're not a psychiatrist?"

"Right now I'm a doctor working in the psychiatry department."

"Well . . . this is not what I was expecting."

"What were you expecting?"

I made a sweeping motion with my arm. "This room is just giving me a bad vibe."

"Why are you so worried about the room?"

"I'm not *worried* about it, but I have a home decor blog, so I pay a lot of attention to spaces. And this room is not a warm or welcoming space. Shouldn't a psychiatrist's office be, like, cozy and comforting?"

"Why would you think that?"

"Why *wouldn't* you think that?"

"I've never really thought about what the room should look like."

"Well, if you're planning to make psychiatry your specialty, you really should. Spaces make people feel things."

"How so?"

Was this dudebro seriously serious right now? I rolled my eyes and kept on even though I didn't want to continue justifying his accusatory questions with legitimate answers.

"Don't worry. The walls aren't, like, communicating with me or anything. I actually know what I'm talking about here."

"And what are we talking about?" Then, before I had time to answer: "Why are we here today, Emily?"

"Not because I think walls talk to me," I said, letting out a dismissive half laugh I hoped would palpably shift the power dynamic in my favor. "Isn't it right there on your little clipboard?"

(Had I made him feel inferior? I hoped I'd made him feel inferior.)

"Okaaaaay . . ." he said. I watched his eyes dart from the top of his wittle clipboard to the bottom and back up again.

(Did he seriously not know why I was there?)

Then: "I can see here . . . you've been feeling sad?"

(Nope, he definitely did not know why I was there.)

Missed diagnosis of ADHD in women and girls may occur when anxiety or depression presents in association with ADHD because symptoms of ADHD may mistakenly be attributed to the coexisting condition.

—Patricia O. Quinn and Manisha Madhoo,
"A Review of Attention-Deficit/Hyperactivity
Disorder in Women and Girls"

Wittle Baby Doctor Clammy Hands must have been referring to the intake form I'd filled out before my Pap a few months earlier. It had the standard questions I always assumed were used to prescreen for postpartum depression. Inquiries like: "In the last week, have you felt a sense of despair?" and "How many days a week do you feel a sense of hopelessness?" I'd forgotten I answered yes and circled "one to four" on a few of those. But each time it was with a caveat that I very clearly wrote in the margins in all caps: "BUT I BLAME TRUMP!!!" and "FUCKING TRUMP'S FAULT!!!"

We were barely a year into that orange piece of shit's term and things were already so bad I can't remember what particular offense had set me off the week of my Pap. It could have been anything, really: the Muslim ban, kids in cages, government shutdowns, Stormy Daniels, fake news, "shithole countries." I was already emotionally exhausted from it all. "The country is going to hell in a tacky Ivanka Trump handbag!" I'd "joke" to friends after a few drinks.

But none of that was why I was there. The notes in the margin were for my doctor—who I knew was on the same page with me ideologically—*not* for diagnostic purposes, thank you very much. In fact, I'd completely forgotten about that form when I asked her for a psych referral so I could get an official ADHD diagnosis.

I let out an exasperated sigh and explained to Resident Dudebro that the sadness was situational and had nothing to do with how I ended up in this Soft Vom–colored interrogation room educating the commenter who obviously didn't read the article.

"Well, that orange piece of shit *is* a monster. If you're not feeling despair right now, there's something wrong with you," I told him without breaking eye contact.

I wondered if Baby Doctor Dudebro was feeling any despair or just cruising through his rotations and ugly rooms without a care in the world.

"I'm here because I'm fairly certain I have ADHD and I'd like to get an official diagnosis."

"What makes you think you have ADHD?"

"What makes you think I don't?"

"Well, that's what we're here to find out," he said as he handed me a clipboard with way too much paper on it. There were twenty pages, at least, and my right hand started to get crampy just looking at it.

"Take all the time you need to fill it out," he said, *not* making a move toward the door.

Okay, so he's just going to sit here and watch me chicken scratch all over this paper? I thought and congratulated myself for not saying it out loud. *Administrative voyeurism, eh? Is that part of the diagnostic process?* (I kinda wish I would have said that one out loud, too, but it's probably a good thing I didn't.)

It is important to move away from the prevalent perspective that ADHD is a behavioural disorder and attend to the more subtle and/or internalised presentation that is common in females. It is essential to adopt a lifespan model of care to support the complex transitions experienced by females that occur

in parallel to change in clinical presentation and
social circumstances.

—Susan Young et al., "Females with ADHD"

This time, I answered more carefully, took the questions a
little more seriously. I didn't want my timely, biting humor to
be used against me later, or sooner than later in a room with no
windows and two doors.

Occasionally, I'd call out a question that couldn't be
answered with a simple yes or no. "This one is really subjective,
especially since it's so vague." And: "So, um, in my twenties
when I was drinking a lot, I guess I had a lot of casual sexual
encounters. But I was young and insecure and living in New
York City. And, like, drinking. *A lot.* Now I'm old and married
and I bet my husband would tell you I don't have *enough* sexual
encounters." (Was I really supposed to get through my entire
mental health history without cracking at least a few jokes? In
addition to windows, the room really needed some levity.)

Every time, his guidance was the same: "Then just answer
yes. If there's any way it could be a yes, then answer yes."

"This feels like a trap," I mumbled under my breath and
then immediately regretted it because that's exactly what a
delusional person would say.

Female patients primarily exhibiting symptoms of
inattentiveness tend to report low levels of arousal and
may be diagnosed with dysthymia rather than ADHD,
women exhibiting combined symptoms with high

energy and impulsivity could be misdiagnosed with bipolar disorder, and girls presenting with anxiety or depressive symptoms may be treated for these disorders without ADHD ever being considered.

—Patricia O. Quinn and Manisha Madhoo,
"A Review of Attention-Deficit/Hyperactivity
Disorder in Women and Girls"

"Have you ever been able to stay up for days without sleep?"

It was the third time the lady with the brunette bob had asked me that and my answer still hadn't changed.

"No!" I snorted back, angrier this time. "Like I've told you twice before, sometimes I stay up late to finish a project if I'm in the zone or on a deadline, but I always end up sleeping later the next day. I have to sleep. I'm a monster if I don't sleep."

"Tell me more about 'the zone,'" she pressed.

"She" was Resident Clammy Hands's attending, an *actual* board-certified psychiatrist.

After I had thoroughly and humorlessly answered all seventy-three-bajillion questions, Baby Houser, M.D., silently scanned them without even raising one of his infuriatingly perfect eyebrows. Then he said, "I'll be right back," before disappearing for what had to be half an hour. When he returned, he was accompanied by a medical student (someone even less qualified than him, yay!) and the attending psychiatrist—a short woman with a blunt brown bob and matching blunt bangs, who apparently believed that if she asked me the same question on repeat, I would change my answer. (Seriously, how was this different from an interrogation room?)

"Emily, I know you think you have ADHD. But we need to run a full psych panel to rule out bipolar disorder first."

"But I've never been depressed," I told her and her side-kicks. "I mean, I was really sad once after a breakup, but my aunt died a few months before that, and my apartment was growing mold, and my super was taking porno pictures in the courtyard instead of fixing the building, and it was winter and everything kind of sucked. But I knew it was temporary and I came out of it."

She explained that bipolar disorder doesn't always present with depression. "We're more concerned with the mania, anyway."

"Mania?"

(*The fuck???*)

"Well, based on your answers here, you do a lot of impulsive shopping. And Doctor Woodridge said you talk really fast."

"That's considered mania?"

"Well, when you also take into account the all-nighters, it could be."

Greater awareness on the part of healthcare professionals regarding the specific symptom profile of ADHD in women and girls is necessary for proper diagnosis and treatment.

—Patricia O. Quinn and Manisha Madhoo,
"A Review of Attention-Deficit/Hyperactivity
Disorder in Women and Girls"

Bad Friend

So this is how it happens, I thought as I hugged my arms in the tiny shower of my Brooklyn pied-à-terre, paralyzed with fear. *This is how seemingly normal people end up on* Dateline.

That dingy little shower felt like the safest place I could be at the time, and I wanted to stay there forever, but I had to catch a flight back to Kansas City soon.

I was not the kind of person who'd have a second home—some months I could barely make the rent on one apartment, let alone two—but not long after I left Brooklyn for Kansas City, I started to wonder if I'd made a terrible decision. As a twenty-eight-year-old trying to make it in media, a move to the Midwest could kill my career. So I posted an ad on Craigslist looking for a cheap part-time room. "Hell, I'd take an oversized closet as long as it has a window and enough space to keep a few clothes and books," I wrote. What I ended up with was beyond my wildest, broke-girl dreams.

I immediately heard from a newly single woman who couldn't quite afford her two-bedroom Windsor Terrace walk-up now that her ex was gone, but she didn't really want a room-mate either. For the low, low cost of $225 a month, utilities included, I could once again have a room in Brooklyn to call my own—complete with a walk-in closet and its own micro-scopic en suite bathroom. It was a better setup than anything I'd had when I lived in the city full time, and with a few extra cocktail-serving shifts—and my flight-attendant cousin's com-panion passes—I managed to make this double life work much longer than anyone in my financial situation should have. Most of the time, I was in Kansas City, but every few months I'd pop back to New York for a week or two. It was amazing, extravagant, and so far outside the scope of my budget it should have been impossible, but I was determined to make it work, so I did.

I was also not the kind of person to be fielding threats from a famous person, yet there I was in the tiny shower of my sec-ond apartment going over all the ways he might try to kill me as the hot water ran out.

And to think it all started because I wanted to get a little exercise.

Almost exactly a year earlier, I'd signed up for a cardio kickboxing class that took place in a park at the ass crack of dawn. Like second homes and celebrity stalkers, mornings and group cardio classes weren't my things, but after leav-ing a walking city for a car city, I needed to do something to move my body. My bright idea was to find something with a set schedule and prepay for a month, thinking it would force me to roll out of bed three days a week and get my mon-ey's worth. Also, I had high hopes that the instructor—a "retired" amateur MMA fighter—would intimidate me into compliance.

When I showed up for my first session, I was surprised to see the instructor hadn't yet arrived. Everyone there was either squishy like me or too tiny to fight other people for fun. Then, at 6:30 a.m. on the dot, a woman no taller than four foot eight with a very long, brassy blonde ponytail (we're talking down to her thighs) turned away from the group of women she'd been chatting with and started barking orders. So I hit the wet grass for the first of many miserable burpees. And that was just the warm-up. It was followed by forty-five agonizing minutes of the kind of kicking I hadn't done since the Indianettes (yep, still cringey), including some that required me to lie flat on my back on the still very wet lawn.

When we *finally* finished, the instructor—we'll call her Helen—insisted we all go to breakfast together. I didn't want to go. I was there to move my body, not make new friends. Plus, I was desperate to put on dry pants.

"I'm broke until my next shift," I told her. I probably should have tried to sound more sheepish, but I wasn't lying; my bank account was overdrawn. Also, my damp leggings were starting to make my butt cheeks itch and I knew it would only get worse the longer I waited.

"No problemo!" Helen practically yelled. "I'll cover you! See you there!" Before I had a chance to protest—to tell her I had to get out of these pants or I would lose my goddamned mind, and also that I didn't want to be out in public with someone who said things like "no problemo"—she ducked into her tiny red sports car and zipped off.

By the time I walked in, she already had a table and coffee. As I approached the table, so did a waitress with a plate of food. Helen was a regular.

Before I sat down, I stuffed a bunch of napkins into the back of my pants to absorb the moisture. Then I ordered coffee and toast. Already, I had the sense that Helen was someone I did not want to feel indebted to.

"You need to eat more than that! It's recovery!" Was she yelling to me? *At* me? To the whole restaurant? She waved down her waitress/friend. "Get this one the Power Omelet. Potatoes, too!"

As we ate our underseasoned eggs and not-crispy home fries, I learned that Helen was also somewhat new-ish to Kansas City. Most recently, she'd lived in LA, where she was the stunt double for a minor character's death scene in a successful movie franchise. A very popular one that I had most definitely watched.

The actor who played the antihero, she told me, was her best friend.

I couldn't tell whether she was lying to impress me or she really believed they were BFFs, but I just sat and nodded and choked down my mediocre free breakfast and wondered how much longer I would have to wait to change my fucking pants.

After the next kickboxing class, I was informed I had to go to breakfast again because now I owed her one. I told her I still didn't have any cash, but she didn't care. It wasn't money she wanted, anyway.

Now, the best way for anyone to ensure we won't be friends is to try way too hard to make it happen. Sure, there's the whole

Groucho Marx "I refuse to join any club that would have me as a member" thing, but also it's just a lot of pressure. If someone is working so hard to be my friend, then what are they going to expect from the friendship? *From me?* It's too much.

Truth be told, I also feel kind of sad for people who try to befriend me because, on paper, I'm objectively a really bad friend. Just ask Melanie, my best friend since first grade. I've known Melanie since I was six and I still forget her birthday nearly every year. The times I do remember, I get the date wrong (it's either October 10 or October 20 and I will never get it straight). I even missed her wedding shower because I accidentally double-booked myself that day, and as I was driving to the home of someone who is a way better friend than I am, I realized it was going to be an hour each way and I had to turn around and head back. Reader, I was her *maid of honor*. Oh, and on her wedding day, I sneaked off to a bar after the ceremony to write my toast. Apparently, I was supposed to be helping her do or undo something with her dress before the reception. If Melanie and I hadn't known each other so long, if we hadn't grown up in the same subsidized housing development with single parents, if I hadn't bitched out every one of her shitty high school boyfriends, if we weren't practically sisters, I'd like to think that—for her sake—she'd have kicked me to the curb by now purely for being such a terrible friend.

Normally, I'd just quietly disengage from (okay, ghost) someone who was trying as hard as Helen was, and if they pressed the issue, I'd tell them the truth: "I can't be the friend you need right now." But I'd already paid for a month of her kickboxing classes and she had paid for two of my breakfasts.

And as I quickly learned, with Helen, every debt begat more debt.

When I tried to quit kickboxing after my prepaid month was up—because I legitimately couldn't afford to keep going— she refused my resignation. But not to worry: I could just pay her whenever, when I had more money. When the transmission went out on my old Volvo and I could no longer put it in reverse, she picked me up in the mornings and took me home. After breakfast, naturally.

Though she wasn't someone I would have chosen to spend time with—and the time I did spend with her sapped every ounce of energy I had—I did appreciate what seemed like generosity back then. And she had started to grow on me, or I started to tolerate her more, and aren't those really the same thing?

Helen was weird and loud and irritating and she didn't always smell great. But she was smarter than I'd originally given her credit for and sometimes funny, too. She also had no shortage of strange talents and interesting stories (even if I thought some of them were complete bullshit). We exchanged gossipy emails about the annoying people in the class. Our dogs had a few playdates. I owed her a lot of money. But then one day I didn't. An "anonymous benefactor" had paid my balance. For fear of feeling indebted to yet another human, I avoided asking too many questions.

A few days later, I got my first email from her "best friend," the movie star.

Helen had been filling him in on the kickboxing hot goss (she often told me they talked three times a day) and now he wanted to dish with me.

Bad Friend **129**

By this point, I'd already seen pictures of them together, so I accepted that they were at least friendly, if not true friends. And one time, I heard his *very recognizable* voice over the phone, so I was confident they weren't catfishing me (though this was 2009 and the term "catfishing" was still about a year away from entering the lexicon). To what end these two weirdos might have been scamming me, I was never sure, and I don't think I'll ever understand their intense but not sexual interest in me.

Things with Celebrity BFF started out normalish enough. Right away we exchanged a few emails. The next day he sent me three more. Then four after that. It felt excessive, but I also enabled it by replying to almost every message right away.

Because as much as I hate to admit it, I was flattered that this hugely famous person wanted to be friends with *me*. More than that, it kind of put to rest my fears that leaving New York meant I was falling off the face of the earth. Sure, maybe snarky bloggers and publishing people would forget about me, but here was this A-list celebrity knocking down my virtual door to be my friend. I'm embarrassed by how much I enjoyed the implicit cachet, though I mostly kept the "friendship" to myself.

Then the email frequency increased. And then increased some more. And these were some long-ass emails! It was completely overwhelming, so I started replying to his forty-line manifestos with a quick sentence or two.

My biggest mistake (or so it seemed at the time) was showing him how to use Google Chat. Every time I opened my computer, there he was with some story of his own woe. This woe, I pointed out to Celebrity BFF, stemmed from his obvious infatuation with Helen (which I did not understand, but I was trying not to judge). And once that was an established truth between us, things just got more intense.

He was longing. He was heartsick. He was sometimes drunk. And after thousands and thousands and *thousands* of words, he told me he wanted me to help him get the girl/retired amateur MMA fighter.

And because I'm a sucker for the chance to plot an elaborate scheme in a very short amount of time—one that demands my intense and undivided attention to the detriment of absolutely everything else in my life—of course, I fucking helped.

This plan of ours involved a surprise trip to Kansas City, a penthouse hotel room, lots of roses (his idea, not mine), and a declaration of love that had been a long time coming. It was cheesy, but so were Helen and Celebrity BFF.

What did or didn't happen between them that night and in the months after is not my story to tell, so I won't. But my story is that I had gotten myself way too involved in the lives of these people I never actively chose to befriend. It wasn't the first time I'd let myself get wrapped up in someone else's drama—because when it feels like Something Big Is About to Happen, I get completely sucked into the vortex and there's no getting off the ride until the graviton has come to a complete stop and my head stops spinning long enough to ask myself, *What the fuck was that?!*

After the events in the penthouse—which were *mostly* positive, I'll tell you that much—communication from Celebrity BFF intensified. And he expected me to be available to him around the clock. Sometimes he'd joke that I'd become his therapist. I wanted to very seriously reply, "Yes, but you can

afford to spend $500 an hour on a real mental health profes-
sional, yet I can barely pay my rent(s) and here you are keeping me from making twenty cents a word." But I never said
it, so he just kept going. Less often, when he wasn't being so
self-absorbed, he'd thank me for listening. And every once in a
while, he'd have boxes of fancy muffins sent to my apartment. I
would have rather had my time back, but they were really good
muffins and I needed to eat, so . . .

As I relayed all of this to a not-famous friend over drinks
one night, I realized how truly fucked up the entire situation
was. How much of my time and energy it was wasting. How I
didn't owe these people anything (well, beyond a few hundred
bucks).

I can be a real asshole when I want to be, but I will also
do just about anything to avoid a confrontation that I know
might hurt someone's feelings. So instead of ripping off the
Band-Aid, I decided to slowly back away from our dysfunctional
throuple—which really just meant taking longer and longer to
reply to his emails and her texts. I also finally—finally!—quit
kickboxing. I did it over email, in the middle of the night, and
before I hit Send, I signed up for a twelve-month gym membership so I'd have something to point to when Helen tried to force
me back yet again. (I used that gym membership maybe seven
times, but I joined for the emotional benefits, anyway.)

Neither seemed to get the hint. Or if they did, they didn't
care. So I did something I'm not proud of but also a little
proud of because it was kind of brilliant—though much cru-
eler than simply telling Celebrity BFF I no longer wanted to
be friends.

At the time, I was writing an advice column for a now-defunct local lifestyle publication. I knew he read it, so one week, I made up and answered my own question about how a person goes about dumping a friend. Instead of vanishing from my life like a normal insecure weirdo would after reading such a blatantly pointed piece, he rattled off many, many angry emails that opened with lines like, "You're trying to get rid of *me*?!"

The first time I responded I apologized for how I'd handled things and explained that I'm a lifelong terrible friend and that the people I've maintained friendships with don't expect me to be constantly available (*which is why they're still my friends, hello!*). I told him my work and social life and bank account had suffered because I'd spent so much time online with him. I told him what I should have said back when he was sending a mere three emails a day: I couldn't be the friend he needed. I also thanked him for all the muffins, which probably wasn't necessary. But they *were* really good muffins.

My reply made things worse. His emails became more aggressive and more frequent. I should have just stopped engaging, but I felt crippling guilt for hurting this person, so I kept trying to defuse the situation with apologies and explanations.

I would soon be heading to my place in Brooklyn for a week, and he'd known about the trip since I planned it months earlier. But I needed a break, so I not-so-politely told him to leave me alone while I was gone. That's when he started with the vague-but-terrifying threats like, "Do you have any idea who I am and what I can do? I will ruin your life. I will destroy everything you care about. You have no idea what I'm capable of." And that was just in one email. In subsequent messages he said he'd never been so angry in his life and that what was happening was like a nuclear reaction he couldn't control.

Between the threats, he'd accuse me of baiting him, of hurting him with my "insults," of destroying *his* life. None of that lined up with the reality of the situation, but he was right about one thing: I had no idea what he was capable of. Which is why, in my tiny Brooklyn shower, on the day I was supposed to fly back to Kansas City, I started to imagine all the ways he might use his money and power to kill me. He knew where I lived. *Will he send a hitman to my apartment?* He knew what car I drove (by then, I'd replaced my first old Volvo with one that went forward *and* backward). *Can you even put a car bomb in a 1991 Volvo?* It also wouldn't have been that hard to figure out which flight I was on. *How much money does it take to make a plane go down in a cornfield?? Probably less than I think.*

As I packed, I went over all the things I'd done wrong, all the times I should have cut off communication sooner. I'd certainly been too eager to chat in the beginning, and this wasn't the first time being an, er, enthusiastic conversationalist had sent the wrong signal. Usually, though, it was a handyman, a cable guy, or an exterminator mistaking my genuine gratitude for their service as romantic interest. Those incidents usually resulted in unwanted texts and other out-of-line communication—which was annoying and also infuriating—but that kind of stuff was easy enough to ignore. This was the first time someone had literally threatened me. It was also the first time the person in question wasn't trying to bed me. And, yes, I guess I'd done a little more than chat enthusiastically. I'd also been an insensitive coward when I wanted to end the friendship. But none of that justified the threats and harassment. *From someone regularly making the rounds on the late-night circuit.*

At one point, it crossed my mind to call the police, but I knew no one would believe me (I could hardly believe it myself), which made the whole thing more frightening.

I was relieved when I had to turn off my phone on the plane. But when we reached cruising altitude, I got sweaty in the places I do when I get nervous, including that spot where my ass meets my thighs. (Was there no end to the wet butt these people would inflict upon me?!) When the seatbelt sign went off, I tried to calm my nerves with the idea that the person threatening me was not, in fact, Liam Neeson's character in *Taken* and as far as I knew didn't have any particular set of skills beyond acting. And I swear on my kids' lives he wasn't Liam Neeson either. No, Celebrity BFF was just a sad, troubled man who needed more from a friendship than I was willing to give. He also desperately needed a bona fide therapist. And probably some anger management classes, too.

Obviously, my plane didn't get shot down, but when I landed I had a voicemail from my half-sister, Heather, letting me know our dad had suffered a second heart attack.

I couldn't deal with being scared for my dad and scared for my own personal safety at the same time, and I hoped that if I relayed this development to Celebrity BFF he'd have enough decency to leave me alone, at least for a few days. When I opened my email, my iPhone 3G immediately downloaded three new missives. I didn't read any of them, but I did click on one for the sole purpose of responding. I wrote: "I don't care what you do to me. My dad just had a heart attack. Please leave me alone for a while."

I should have known that was too much to ask. In place of scary emails, he started sending gratuitously sympathetic ones. I did my best to ignore them and wrote back just once to make clear I needed some time and space not only to deal with my dad but also to process the threats. Amazingly, he went quiet.

A few days later, a box of muffins showed up at my apartment. Some other perishables were in there, too, including fresh fruit. I ate the muffins—but only because they were sealed, and really good. There was no way I was touching that fucking fruit, though. Death by poisoned apple would be too perfect an ending to this story. Also, I really, *really* hate fruit.

I never acknowledged the possibly poisoned gift. I just wanted to be done with him, with her, with all the drama. But it didn't take long for the nasty emails to start pouring in again (which, in retrospect, likely wouldn't have happened if he believed he'd successfully poisoned me, so I guess those apples were safe after all).

In the last message he sent before I blocked him for good, he wrote: "You do care way too much that I'm [insert name that would make you lose your shit here]."

Tramp Stamp

Are you a Cowboys fan?" the massage therapist asked.

"A whatta what?" What was she asking me? And why? And why during *a massage*?

"Your star," she said cheerily. "You have the Dallas Cowboys logo tattooed on your back."

Most of the time I forget I have a lower-back tattoo. And I cannot go any further without pointing out that it is absolutely not a logo for a sports team—or anything else for that matter. It's just a fairly simple geometric shape with five points. One that many entities—mostly in Texas—have co-opted for their brands. It was also the most basic, most affordable way to cover my original lower-back tattoo, which is why it's slightly off-kilter.

"What's the significance, then?" Tanya pressed as she dug her elbow into the muscle under my shoulder blade.

This has always been my least-favorite tattoo inquiry. Because about 50 percent of my ink has no sentimental value whatsoever. There's a peony design on my upper right arm that's there because I thought it would make a gorgeous partial sleeve. I planned it for months. There's a star on the inside of my left ankle because I like the shape of a star. There are three hollow stars on the back of my left shoulder because, well, you know. Those half-inch stars look like prison tattoos now, but I felt pretty badass when I got them at age nineteen. The dogwood blossoms on my chest were a thirtieth birthday present to myself and that piece does have some significance—dogwood is the official tree of Missouri. And until I wrote that last sentence, I forgot the dogwood is covering up three small black stars I had inked just above my right boob while visiting my cool Aunt Susie in Atlanta when I was nineteen or twenty.

I find it so strange that everyone thinks a tattoo has to *mean* something when it's my most meaningful tattoos—the emotionally driven, hastily designed ones—that look the worst.

The Wilco lyric I had put on the back of my neck because I was convinced "Jesus, Etc." had saved my life after a devastating breakup? Now it looks like somebody splattered water on a drawing done in washable black marker. I got that one the same night Jo and I got our matching sister tattoos on our inner left forearms. Mine says IN JO I TRUST and hers says IN EMILY I TRUST, and though Jo's still looks fairly sharp, mine has absorbed into my pale, forty-year-old skin enough to now appear as if it were done by Big Red in Cell Block Three. Then there's the tattoo right above that one, closer to the crease of my elbow. I got it ten years later, on a whim, an hour after the 2017 solar eclipse. I was so high on the dopamine of watching the moon pass through the center of the earth's shadow in a cornfield with a bunch of strangers that I raced back to the city and found the only tattoo parlor with an opening for walk-ins. And even though I *knew* I shouldn't let the guy with the face ink—who seemed to be actively high on much more than dopamine—take a needle to my skin for what was supposed to be a perfect hollow circle surrounded by delicate shading, I had to have it. I'm at peace with it enough now to admit that it looks like shit.

I used to be proud that, unlike many people my age, I never desired a Chinese symbol (with deep meaning, of course). But would it really have been any worse than getting drama masks tattooed onto the small of my back?

So Much Potential

He was your favorite teacher and he looked pretty much how you'd expect a high school English teacher in the nineties to look. He was shorter than most of the grown men you knew and he had thinning hair, crooked teeth, and a prominent, pointy nose that looked like it should have been crooked, but wasn't. Every day he wore some variation on the same thing: a sweater vest over a plaid shirt, khaki pants rolled at the ankle, and brown leather slip-on shoes you suspected he bought on a trip to Europe. Maybe Belgium or Germany, but you only thought that because they reminded you of Birkenstocks. Now that you think about it, they probably were Birkenstocks and they probably weren't purchased overseas.

When your favorite teacher spoke, it sounded like he had a frog in his throat and it was the perfect complement to his dry sense of humor. Other kids thought he was either boring or unpredictably mean, but you were in on the joke and that's part of why you liked him so much. His best bits were the fake meltdowns during which he'd scatter his papers all over his desk in exaggerated fits of frustration or throw the chalkboard eraser across the room where it would land in a dramatic cloud of dust. Slightly less entertaining were his offhand remarks about school administration, the government, and required texts, but you thoroughly enjoyed those, too.

He taught English, Russian, and Broadcasting, and you spent a lot of time with him because Broadcasting was one of your favorite classes (second only to Theater, which you obnoxiously spelled with the *e* at the end back then). When selecting your junior year electives, the guidance counselor reminded you that you needed two years of the same foreign language to get into most colleges, and because you had exactly zero foreign language credits, you signed up for your favorite teacher's Russian class, too. By the end of the first semester, you could recite the entire Russian alphabet and put together a few remedial sentences—one being "I like alcohol." It was pronounced something like "al-go-gol."

Not at all shockingly, Russian wasn't a hit among high school kids in Middle America and because of dwindling enrollment for an already unpopular subject, the district discontinued the class the summer before your senior year. You thought you were seriously screwed until you convinced your favorite teacher, along with whoever signed off on such things, to let you do an independent study so you could fulfill your stupid credit requirements and just go to college already.

Through it all, you hoped (and kind of assumed) that your favorite teacher appreciated your quirks as much as you did his. That he saw your chronic lateness, sporadic truancy, and unpredictable bursts of intense enthusiasm as the charming traits of a brilliant creative who had bigger things to worry about than high school popularity contests or the rigid schedules set by the rule makers you both rolled your eyes at. You also assumed that he didn't really care that you were no longer actually studying anything independently since he wasn't giving you much trouble, or much homework.

It's not like you'd ever have any use for Russian, anyway (there's no way you could have known you'd sign a lease on a Brighton Beach rental a few years later). And to be fair, it was your senior year, and other than those damn Russian credits, you'd more than fulfilled your graduation requirements. Plus, wasn't senioritis a normal part of adolescent development? Maybe losing all interest in high school meant that you were normal after all. Maybe.

Then one Saturday in March or April, you're at school after a chamber choir competition, and as you're about to head out, you remember to grab a book you were supposed to have read cover to cover weeks earlier. The hallway that houses your locker is quiet without its usual swarms of horny teenagers, and it's depressingly dark with the fluorescent lights turned off. You've done so many extracurricular activities in your four years there that it doesn't feel weird to you, but you're still startled when you turn to leave and your favorite teacher and his wife step out of a classroom to your left. It's not even his classroom and, until now, you've never seen him there on a weekend. You've never seen his wife, period.

"Oh, hi!" he says as if he's surprised to see you. As if he'd just randomly run into you right by your locker on a Saturday afternoon. As if this were a genuine coincidence. "I want you to meet my wife."

Your favorite teacher's wife cheerily introduces herself and then her tone becomes more somber. "I hear so much about all the great things you do. I also hear that you miss class a lot and when you are there, you're late."

There's more, too—something about not following through with things and something else about having lots of potential—but you don't hear it. Your ears are already ringing and you can feel your face turning that almost-neon-pink shade it does when you're exceedingly embarrassed. Your eyes start to fill with tears and you want to cry or at least defend yourself, but you don't, because what can you say? She's not wrong.

"I hate to do that to you," your favorite teacher says when his wife is done. And you notice his eyes are welling up, too. "It's just that you have a chance to really make something of yourself and I don't want to see you mess that up."

You can't remember how you left things in the hallway and you don't mention this encounter to anyone until you're supposed to write a college essay about "the greatest lesson you ever learned." Though you're starting to wonder if the only thing you really learned was that maybe your favorite teacher didn't see you the way you thought he did—like everyone else, he believed you needed to try harder—and you write about this moment. Because even while earning a fancy New York liberal arts degree (that you will never, ever, ever pay off), you don't yet understand the difference between big life lessons and shame.

They stay with you—the conversation, the essay, your favorite teacher, his wife, and definitely those student loans—and you remember them when you're feeling bad about yourself because you messed up something yet again. She wasn't wrong. He wasn't wrong. And you didn't learn a damn thing, did you?

Years later, you become Facebook friends with your favorite teacher. It's a little weird, but it's nice to reconnect. When his wife dies, you send him the essay you wrote in college, as a tribute of sorts, but you edit out the part about his long nose and crooked teeth because while you find his distinctive features endearing, you don't want to hurt his feelings—especially not when he's already in pain—and because even now, as an adult, you still seek his validation.

He writes such a heartfelt response, your eyes well up with tears again. They're happier tears now. But you don't have the energy to reply in kind, so you tell yourself you'll do it later. Too much time passes—months and then years. Whenever you think of it you feel guilty for not responding, so you just keep . . . not responding.

Nearly twenty years after the not-so-chance meeting by your locker, when you have a spouse and a house and a kid and a résumé that would be ten pages long if you ever wanted to get a real job again, you get a diagnosis that explains so much. Now you have a reason to finally reply to his last message. This time you do it without any shame. You tell him you're surprised none of the adults in your life ever saw it or tried to figure out what was going on, but that maybe he did see it.

He writes back immediately:

> What I saw, and what my wife confirmed, was
> your glorious potential. Maybe it was fueled

somewhat by that restless energy that gets called some scientific name, but however you decide to address it, and only you can make the best choice for you, I have every confidence that you'll find a way to channel it for good, your own as well as other people's.

It's not a perfect response (maybe there is no perfect response). But it's not wrong, either.

A Tale of Two Summers

I. Basket Case, 2018

It was the best of times, it was the worst of times. I'd recently received an official diagnosis of ADHD and was thrilled to have an explanation (and medication) for what I had so long believed to be a vast collection of character flaws. But Kyle and I were still fighting pretty regularly. Life as we knew it had yet to be upended by an apparently never-ending pandemic. But we weren't even halfway through the era of that orange piece of shit and his reign of racism and destruction. Bad men were finally being called out for their bad behavior. But one of them was about to be nominated for the Supreme Court. I'd just poured all my rage, anxiety, and money into a renovation of my ugly kitchen. But I was broke. And not just cash poor—I'd nearly maxed out three credit cards to pay for "a few cosmetic updates" that turned into all-new upper shelving, a brand-new sink complete with a champagne bronze pull-down faucet (and matching flange!), new countertops, and a last-minute range hood purchase that really tied the room together if I do say so myself.

Because moderation is not my strong suit, and because more often than not my fights with Kyle began over money, I attempted to course correct with a self-imposed three-month spending freeze. I declared it the Summer of No Spending and decided I wouldn't buy anything that wasn't food, drink, or otherwise a necessity. Did this mean I could order a fancy $14 cocktail when we were out? Well, yes. But it's important to stay hydrated, especially in the summer. I could not, however, buy a $14 tube of red lipstick, a warmer-toned light bulb just because the hastily purchased "daylight" bulb gave the kitchen all the ambiance of an operating room, or a cute keychain at Target no matter how cute (seriously, why is everything at Target so goddamn cute?).

When I relayed my plan to Kyle (leaving out the part about pricey cocktails, of course), he rolled his eyes.

"There is no way you can go an entire summer without buying anything," he said. "Remember a few years ago when you started a blog dedicated to frugal living? How long did that last?"

"A while," I retorted, half offended at his lack of faith in me and half not ready to accept that he was probably right. "And I had lots of followers, too. But then we bought the house and I had to buy stuff for it."

"Emily . . ."

As much as I wanted him to be wrong, I knew he wasn't. I'd always been bad at sticking to any kind of budget, even one with a catchy name. And I could already tell medication alone wasn't going to shut down my urge to shop. But just as I was about to admit defeat, I had an idea.

"Okay! Maybe it's unreasonable to think I won't buy any-thing," I offered. "So I'll allow myself one exception: thrift stores."

I swear to the Flying Spaghetti Monster that when I made this fateful suggestion, I had not yet seen the Instagram Post About the Owl Basket. But once I saw it—maybe two weeks after codifying the terms of my Summer of No Spending—things spiraled out of control. Quickly.

The Instagram Post About the Owl Basket was just that: a post, on Instagram, about a decorative basket in the shape of an owl. Though I already considered myself a semi-pro thrifter, I had decided to follow a bunch of new-to-me vintage sellers (I guess for shopping inspiration when I wasn't supposed to be spending any money?). One reseller in Chicago had posted a shot of her own thrifted owl basket and I happened upon the photo when stalking her feed for the first time.

I've always had a thing for owl decor—particularly of the vintage variety—and this seemingly rare piece felt like a thrifting challenge. It was all I could think about. More than I wanted an owl basket for myself, I wanted to find an owl bas-ket. And somehow I knew there was one in Kansas City just waiting for me to rescue it from a dusty shelf. I lasted all of ninety minutes before abandoning whatever piece of sponsored content I was writing for a frozen food manufacturer, hopped in my car, and drove west toward the suburbs.

One of the benefits of living in the Midwest is that you're almost guaranteed to find good vintage in a thrift store. So I was confident I'd eventually find the owl, or something very close. I was so eager to start rummaging that before I made it out of the city, I stopped by what amounted to a junk shop with a housewares section crammed into one corner of a very hot and humid second floor. I knew the less organized (and worse smelling) the store, the better chance I had of discovering hidden treasure.

Overcome with excitement, I practically ran from my car and made a beeline up the creaky, stained stairs to the baskets. If this had been a regular thrift store visit, I wouldn't have been able to resist stopping by the dusty glassware shelf first, but because I was being propelled by my inner basket-finding force, I kept my eye on the prize. I was there for decorative baskets and decorative baskets alone, preferably in the shape of adorable animals.

As I searched the shelves with one hand, I cradled three gorgeous shallow round baskets in the other. When I noticed they were only sixty cents each, I grabbed three more in complementary sizes and weaves. Then I set them aside and started to really dig around the outskirts of the basket section—as if I would magically unearth an owl basket on the very first stop on the very first day of my basket journey.

Then I picked up a thin metal tray adorned with polar bears and the Coca-Cola logo and saw a motherfucking owl basket. Except it wasn't just any owl basket. It was *the* owl basket. Yes, mere minutes into my search, I had found the exact same owl basket that, two hours earlier, I had seen for the very first time in the Instagram Post About the Owl Basket.

I went to the register to make it official, then rushed home to begin mounting my new-to-me wall art. With no plan and a mixing bowl full of random hardware (the bowl also held a tube of reddish-orange lipstick, a sewing needle, and a single, ancient OB tampon), I picked what seemed like the perfect place for the owl and tacked him to the wall. Then I started arranging the other baskets around him.

Have baskets always been this beautiful? This artful? I wondered as I hammered nails into the old plaster wall, then pulled them out when I realized they needed to move about an inch to the left or right. *And how is it that a basket's beauty is enhanced by the presence of other baskets?*

Ten minutes later, I was pretty content with my new basket wall, but it was missing something. And that something was clearly more baskets.

I was missing something, too. Finding the owl basket from the Instagram Post About the Owl Basket had been way too easy. My quest for bird-shaped fiber art should have taken me all around town. It should have had me tearing through grimy shelf after grimy shelf after grimy shelf while adrenaline coursed through my veins. Ideally, this quest would have taken me out of town as well, to the kind of flea market that pops up in Middle of Nowhere, Missouri, twice a year. (And a flea market is technically a giant outdoor thrift store, so I wouldn't even be straying from the Summer of No Spending.)

Evidently, my original goal had been too attainable, my focus too narrow, my gratification too instant—even for my impulsive, dopamine-seeking brain. And really, aren't we all supposed to be focusing on the journey instead of the destination or whatever? While I'm sure that clichéd quote (and its myriad variations) is meant to inspire contentment, in this instance, I would argue that I was not given ample opportunity to enjoy the journey.

The only solution was more baskets. All the baskets.

Over the next few weeks, I made my way to those suburban thrift stores I'd missed on my first day of basket hunting, and then I went to other stores. At every stop, I loaded my cart with anywhere from three to ten decorative baskets and each acquisition made me more excited about what I might find next. Sometimes I got so worked up about basket hunting that my heart would race on the drive to an unfamiliar shop.

I tried to make homes for all of them, but decorative baskets don't serve any practical purpose since they're too shallow to hold much of anything. Still, I hung them where I could: on the burgeoning basket wall in the dining room, in the living room, in the kitchen, in the bathroom, in the bedroom I shared with Kyle, and in my toddler's bedroom, too. The baskets that had a little more depth became receptacles for unopened mail (of which I had plenty). When one got too full, I shoved the whole thing in a closet and replaced it with something similar from my ever-expanding stock.

It wasn't long before baskets started to pile up on the dining room table, in my office, and in the garage. At this point, we weren't yet using the attic floor of our house, and because the stairs were behind a door, I stored baskets in the stairway, too.

"Remind me: What's the plan for all these baskets?" Kyle asked one night when he came home and found a stack of baskets on the kitchen counter.

"Babe. Baskets are all over Instagram right now. I can sell collections for, like, eighty bucks," I told him as if his Instagram feed were also filled with pictures of well-styled basket walls. "Seriously—every time I post about them on my Instagram stories, I get messages from people asking me to sell them a set."

"Okay . . . then will you please start selling them so they stop taking over our house?"

I'd dabbled in vintage sales back when I was blogging about frugality, and a few years after that I had my own line of potty-mouth greeting cards, so I already had an Etsy storefront. I was also a professional prop stylist and photographer, so I knew how to stage something to make it sell for way more than it was worth. What I'd forgotten, however, was what a huge pain in the ass it was to list vintage items for sale since every element must be measured and the condition of each has to be described in detail. Flaws and blemishes also needed their own close-ups and if I was going to have a store full of basket collections, I'd have to style each set a little differently so every picture didn't look exactly the same. And then there was the whole shipping issue to consider. Getting anything in the mail had always been a real challenge for me.

I ended up selling exactly one collection to a local Instagram follower. And only because she never asked me about measurements and met me at a coffee shop to complete the transaction. Because she was so accommodating, I gave her a discount, too.

A few weeks after I made my basket fortune of sixty-five dollars, I learned my house was going to be featured on a popular home decor blog. I had about two months to get the entire main floor photo-ready, and it wasn't gonna be cheap.

The first step was shoving all those fucking baskets onto shelves in the garage. Except for the owl, who is still perched on the dining room wall.

II. Plant Lady, 2022

"What are you buying?" Kyle asked as soon as I answered the phone.

"Nothing for the front. I promise!" My tone was probably a little too quick and defensive, which I know makes it sound like I'm up to something.

He had decided to pop by the house for lunch and, on the way, he spotted my brown RAV4 parked in front of the garden center up the street.

Because I have a history of acting on every whim that has anything to do with decor or aesthetics (and most other whims, too), and because Kyle has a history of complaining that I never include him in anything, we have some sore spots in our home—and I'm talking actual spots in and around the house that can stir up hurt feelings and resentment. There's the kitchen I renovated without him, the sectional I bought without him, the nursery I painted without him, the dining table I swapped without him, the bar I got rid of and replaced without him, and an entirely different bar I mounted on the wall after getting rid of the second bar without him. Then there was the deck I accidentally spent a very hot, hellish week staining, then stripping, then staining again (all because I'd been a little too overzealous cleaning some algae from a railing). That, too, was a solo mission.

But save for the Great Deck Stain Spiral of 2021, I spent weeks—if not months or years—trying to get Kyle on board for all those updates. And as I learned not long after we closed on what I believed to be our "project house," when it comes to home improvements, he is the tortoise and I am the hare. Though he'd probably deny it, I'm pretty sure Tortoise Kyle would have been very content spending the rest of our lives in the house's 2013 "as is" condition.

By the summer of 2022, the sorest spot on our property— and in our marriage—was the grass-bare one along the front of our porch. Kyle and I had long agreed that it was in desperate need of landscaping, but every time we got close to taking action, things would go downhill at the last minute. It usually ended with me in tears at the idea of waiting one second longer to just fucking plant something already and Kyle accusing me of steamrolling him—yet again. This cycle had repeated itself every July for seven or eight years.

But the week before he saw my car at the garden center, we had finally (finally!) worked out a plan. By some miracle of the Marriage Gods, we'd managed to make real headway by creating a brick border for our imminent bed of bushes—together. I was so into collaborating that I was happy to scrap my original design in favor of his more practical, spacious plot.

He felt included. It felt good to me, too.

So there was no way in hell I was picking out plants for the front yard without him. But also, I wasn't not buying plants for the front yard. I was just . . . buying plants. All the plants—though mostly the kind that like shade since the areas most in need of beautification don't get very much sun. The bushes and ground cover I was stockpiling behind my shed— not exactly purposely where Kyle wasn't likely to see them— could have gone anywhere. Our double city lot was our oyster, and I was ready to fill it with boxwoods, hostas, creeping Jenny, muhly grass, and more.

If it sounds like I know a lot about plants (specifically shade-loving plants for USDA Hardiness Zone 6a), it's because I'd recently become obsessed with lawn care, which quickly spiraled into me wanting to fill the front and back yards with gorgeous perennials. In a matter of weeks, I'd gone from living in the house with the shittiest yard on the block (seriously, we once got a citation and a $500 fine for overgrown grass) to researching Master Gardener certification.

"I've decided I want to be an eccentric old lady who's known for her gaaaaaardens," I'd announced to Kyle a few days before this most recent plant-buying excursion. "And now that I'm forty, I better get a move on!"

And get a move on I did.

If Kyle always came home for lunch, he might have noticed that it was the third day that week my car was parked in front of the plant store. And if I was willing to fully combine our finances and if I was less secretive about my spending, he'd have known that I had already blown through the "fun money" I hold back from each of my paychecks and that I was now putting plants—plants that thus far had no designated home—on a credit card.

My brain was in nonstop plant mode, and there was nothing I could do to stop it. I just needed more plants. As many plants as money (and my dwindling available credit line) could buy.

First came evergreen shrubs. Mostly I bought boxwoods, even though I've always found them a little too formal. They don't mind the shade or Midwestern winters and they get big fast—three of the most important features when you're trying to take your yard from "barren wasteland" to Grandma's Gorgeous Garden in a matter of weeks. But before my boxwoods ever made it into the ground, I went back for flowering shrubs (not to be confused with plain old flowers) to add color and texture. When Kyle saw my car in front of the shop, I had returned yet again to buy fillers—a dismissive term for surprisingly pricey ornamental grasses and obscure ferns.

As far as I was concerned, the more plants I could acquire, the easier it would be to make it look like I'd been tending to my gaaaaaardens for years—and that was one hundred percent the look I was after.

Though I'd gone down more than one rabbit hole reading about which plants would do well on our challenging lot, I had failed to make any sort of plan for where my acquisitions would go. Once I started arranging the little plastic pots in the first two garden beds I'd built and prepped near my shed, I quickly realized I had more plants than I knew what to do with. Impulsive Plant Purchases of Summers Past taught me that if I didn't get them in the ground soon, they'd die.

Kyle regularly tells me that I'm bad at presenting ideas to him, mostly because I skip the part where I acknowledge his wants and needs—or my own history of what he calls "acting unilaterally"—before detailing my nonnegotiable plans for an often elaborate or expensive project.

"You bring me in at step nineteen, then pretend I have any say in anything," he explained once when I asked him to help me understand his frustration. "Then you show me two nearly identical shades of white paint and act like I'm making real decisions."

I knew I had to tread lightly here. But I was also emboldened by the fact that I had at least three (if not four or five) things working in my favor. For starters, Kyle was already fully on board for this landscaping project and had helped make most of the preliminary decisions. And though I hadn't purchased any plants with a specific patch of soil in mind, I had purchased an impressively wide variety of shade-loving shrubs (easy to do when you buy just about every shade-loving option in the store). Perhaps most importantly, we were in the middle of a miserable heat wave.

"So . . . you know I love spending money and I really would love for the two of us to go plant shopping together," I told Kyle after breakfast the day before we were supposed to go plant shopping together. Everyone was full and in a good mood (the best time to have hard conversations). "But it's going to be a million degrees and the boys are going to lose their minds in there and then I'll get frustrated and hot and overstimulated and I won't be the best version of myself and, well . . . what if we just go 'shopping' from my selection?"

I waited for him to say something, but he didn't.

"Because I think maybe I bought a few too many plants."

The ADHD Taxman Cometh

"This looks scary," I said as I handed Kyle a piece of mail from the Missouri Department of Civil Process. "I bet it's a jury summons."

As someone with a history of accounts going into collections, I was relieved the foreboding envelope wasn't addressed to me for a change and proceeded to brag to my husband that I'd only been called for jury duty one time, in the early aughts.

"It was, like, six months after I moved to Brooklyn," I chirped. "I lost the paper and then I never heard from them again!"

Except I probably did hear from them again and I just didn't know it because I don't open my mail—which, it turns out, was the reason the government was now sending scary notices to my husband. Well, that and he was the one with a real job, so he had actual wages that could be garnished to settle my state tax debt from 2017.

The letter that was very much not a jury summons said that with interest and penalties, I owed the Missouri Department of

Revenue $3,769.03. Plus whatever I owed for 2018, 2019, 2020, and 2021, which I hadn't yet filed though the April 18, 2022, deadline was quickly approaching.

For the record, I'm a person who believes in paying taxes—so much so that when Boomers hurl "socialist" at me as an insult on Facebook, I enthusiastically click the heart reaction. I just happen to be really bad at *filing* my taxes. And when I finally get myself motivated or terrified enough to do that part (which is technically just locating and scanning a million different 1099s and receipts to send to my tax guy), I never have enough money in my checking account to pay what I owe.

Because I've always been bad at paperwork and money management—and very aware of my shortcomings in this particular area—years ago I set up auto payments so I could attempt to stay somewhat on top of my tax debts without having to think much about it. Once a month my bank would auto-magically mail a $250 check to the IRS and, I thought, a $100 check to the state of Missouri.

"It's enough to keep me from going to debtors' jail," I occasionally joked to Kyle, who never laughed when I said it.

Except I apparently never finished setting up the Missouri payment (and never noticed it wasn't processing), so as far as somebody behind a desk in Jefferson City was concerned, I was not only behind on my taxes, I was making zero effort to get caught up. I also wasn't responding to any of their correspondence, so they were left with no choice but to garnish my husband's wages. And it was all my fault.

Spend enough time in ADHD forums or even just a few minutes scrolling #ADHDTikTok and you'll see the term

"ADHD tax" pop up with some regularity. It's a made-up term for a very real problem: the extra costs incurred as a consequence of executive dysfunction. In addition to penalties, late fees, and garnished wages, ADHD tax might mean paying an impound lot to get your car back because you thought it was Tuesday but really it was Wednesday and you parked on the wrong side of the street. It's spending half your paycheck on fresh vegetables only to forget you bought them—until you smell them rotting in the bottom of the fridge. It's having to take an unpaid day off of work to get a new driver's license and debit cards because you lost your wallet yet again. My personal ADHD tax liability also includes a $4,000 emergency plumbing repair from the time a storm blew out our hundred-year-old terracotta water line two days after I let the coverage policy expire. Weeks earlier, I'd told Kyle I'd take care of it, then the renewal form got buried on my desk (to be fair to me, I also had a newborn and my car had recently been totaled in a hit-and-run, but still). We didn't have a cool four grand laying around, so it went on a credit card. Cha-ching, cha-ching, cha-ching.

Beyond the more obvious financial losses, ADHD tax can also be used to describe opportunity costs like getting denied for a mortgage or an apartment as a result of a low credit score, missing your favorite band when they come to town because you put the wrong date for the ticket presale in your calendar, and losing hours of your life to phone calls with billing departments. Those scenarios almost always have their own financial consequences, too: paying double for a concert ticket because you have to buy it from a scalper, shelling out for a motel or rental car or second plane seat because you missed your flight, and even knowingly signing the contract on a predatory loan or lease because, after all of your missteps, it's your only option.

But the worst part isn't the money (though that's hugely stressful); it's the shame.

When I pictured my life at forty, I never imagined I'd still be living paycheck to paycheck. Avoiding calls from unknown numbers because there might be a debt collector on the other end. Panicking when a freelance check is late. Discussing with my husband whether to pay the day care bill or the electric bill this week, then fighting over paper towels because no matter how broke we are, *it's never acceptable to buy patterned paper towels, Kyle!*

And because I'm a seemingly successful person who shouldn't be in this precarious financial situation at this ripe middle age, I go deeper into the hole to make it look like I have my shit together. Rather than admit to anyone I'm broke, I'll gladly bust out a high-interest credit card for a friend's birthday dinner. Also on that card? Plane tickets and hotel rooms for relatives' weddings and funerals, a day care bill here, a tank of gas there, and when times are really tough, plain white paper towels. Because at this particular junction, a 19 percent APR is preferable to letting the world see how much of a financial failure I still am—though I have a family, a job, and a house.

The house, by the way, was *only* possible because, not long after we got married, Kyle received a small inheritance from a great uncle. It wasn't life-changing money, but it allowed us to pay off our wedding debt and put a modest down payment on a modest Midwestern bungalow. We also had to use a little to take care of one of my collections accounts that would have prevented us from getting approved for a mortgage.

"Just because you're poor doesn't mean you have to *look* poor" is a thing my mom used to say. And it's probably one of the many reasons I never stood a chance financially.

Even without ADHD, the economic cards were stacked against me. I was a free-lunch kid who grew up in subsidized housing. My parents divorced when I was three, and when my mom got the child support check every other week, she would treat herself. I'm not saying she never bought food because she usually did, but purses and shoes were her things. Making sure her kids always had what they needed? Not so much. She was even less attentive to our needs once we were old enough to kinda sorta take care of ourselves. I started working when I was fourteen (as soon as I was legally allowed) so I could buy trendy gel pens and Doc Martens that would make me look "not poor." I also had to purchase things like deodorant, shampoo, makeup, and hopefully a car to get back and forth to my job since my mom was often nowhere to be found when I needed a ride.

Fueled by desperation for a better life and a few small scholarships and Pell grants, I made my way to college in New York. Where I got my first tax hit.

By my junior year of college, I was tired of scrambling for the documentation I needed to fill out my FAFSA, the Free Application for Federal Student Aid (without which it was impossible to get any sort of loan or grant), so I made a big deal of filing my taxes on time. It was a huge pain in the ass because I had, like, four different jobs and no money to hire a preparer, but without financial aid, I wouldn't be able to get enough credits to graduate. And all my life I'd been told that once I had a college degree I'd be able to have a successful career and pay back the loans (I was also promised two-point-five children, flying cars, and world peace). So I gladly signed my name on those promissory notes full of legally binding fine print about compound interest because (1) I had no clue what compound interest was, and (2) it meant I could stay in school. But I couldn't get a loan without a FAFSA and I couldn't complete the FAFSA until I'd filed my tax return.

When my timely tax return was rejected in an equally timely manner, I assumed I'd made a mistake; I'm terrible at numbers and I've never been one to pay close attention to instructions. A financial aid counselor helped me figure out that (on the advice of some guy from her church, I later learned) my mom had claimed me as a dependent so she could get a tax credit even though I was supporting myself in New York City and hadn't lived under her roof or received any help from her since I was sixteen. And because she filed earlier than I did, and had already received (and likely cashed) her refund check, I would never see the paltry refund I was planning to use on textbooks. To make matters worse, I had to *re*-file my taxes.

As much as I would like to blame all of my money problems on my mom's low-level tax fraud, it was really more of a kick-me-when-I-was-down situation because I was already in the red—and in the process of developing my own terrible financial habits.

Scraping together funds each semester was a part-time job in itself, so other bills got shoved into my Drawer of Doom because looking at them made me want to vomit or cry or both. I had every intention of getting up to date with everything when I was able (my con woman days started and ended with Columbia House), but I was never able. As the drawer filled with more threatening letters and collection notices, I became filled with dread and shame, so I transferred the papers into a plastic tub, which went into a closet, and it made me feel so much better about my life (albeit temporarily).

Clearly, my filing system had some major flaws, or maybe it was just one big flaw. I honestly believed I was putting things away "for later," but once something was no longer out in the open, it might as well have been gone forever.

About once a year, I'd have a freak-out about money and decide I was really going to get my shit together ("for good this time!") and I'd spend weeks making spreadsheets and calling collection agencies to set up payment plans. It was a dicey stopgap, and I was continuously robbing Peter to pay Paul, but I was trying. One late freelance check or impulsive purchase and the whole system would implode—which it always did—and I'd go back to shoving collection notices into the Drawer of Doom.

In spite of my debilitating debt and major cash flow problems, I could not stop spending. When I'd get an unexpectedly large tip at the cocktail bar where I worked or deposit a paycheck from one of my other jobs, I was momentarily able to experience what it felt like to have money, even if a profit and loss sheet would have proved otherwise. Having money and giving myself permission to spend it felt *so* good—the complete opposite of most days, which were filled with stress from being beyond broke in one of the most expensive cities in the world. It's not like I was buying $3,000 bags (I wasn't even buying $300 bags), but if I had a little cash, I would not hesitate to treat myself to a fancy coffee or funky necklace from Urban Outfitters. Sometimes it meant I could go out to a nice dinner with a friend and pretend I was a real adult. I felt like such a high roller whenever I didn't have to do math in my head before ordering. Spending money like I had it to spend gave me such a rush that it was easy for me to compartmentalize the idea of my money, even when it meant I might not be able to buy groceries the next day.

Less frequent but perhaps more dangerous were the times I fell in love with a particular sweatshirt or slouchy purse (again, we're not talking Birkin bags here). Once I became fixated on something, there was no way to stop myself from buying it—which could result in me overdrawing my bank account on purpose. For some reason, Bank of America allowed me a $200 overdraft limit and I'm certain that reason was their $35 overdraft fees.

If I had it to do over again, I'd tack all my unpaid bills up on the wall and highlight the balances in neon yellow so I'd be forced to face them every damn day. In addition to a much-needed physical reminder of my myriad debts, the potential shame factor of friends and OkCupid dates seeing my financial messiness might have sent me down a different road. Instead, I stayed on the fiscally unstable path—never able to catch up no matter how many articles I wrote or cocktail shifts I worked. I just got used to putting out fires as a means of survival.

Because I always worked at least a few jobs, it took me six years to finish college. When I left, it was with $50,000 in student loan debt. I was supposed to start paying it back six months after graduation, but at that point, I was still so broke that I was granted a financial hardship forbearance. I didn't entirely understand what that entailed, but I was told I wouldn't have to make payments for a while, which at least meant I could continue to cover rent—while that interest would continue to compound. I ended up consolidating my loans with a graduated repayment plan, and for more than a decade, I made monthly payments between $300 and $600 (auto-drafted, so I wouldn't forget). The bright side? I have a better understanding of compound interest. After paying tens of thousands of dollars toward what I originally borrowed, my balance currently hovers around $75,000. That's $25,000 *more* than I owed when I graduated in 2006.

So now I'm one of those entitled (elder) Millennials with a fancy East Coast liberal arts education they complain about on Fox News. And I will probably never get to retire.

My ADHD diagnosis helped me understand how I got here and allowed me to let go of some (but not all) of the shame. And after years of unpredictable and unreliable income as a freelancer, I have a good job that I love doing (for now, anyway), but I'm in such a deep hole that most of what I earn goes toward debt. I'm still really bad at managing my money and filing my taxes. And when I'm feeling overwhelmed and stressed about finances, I still shove scary letters into a drawer so I can relax enough to enjoy dinner with my family—which means there's probably another big issue on the horizon.

I have stopped putting unnecessary shit on credit cards, though. Mostly because of the most recent scary letter to land in my mailbox. It was from the IRS's collection agency—addressed to me this time—letting me know I owed the federal government $50,000. Nearly half of it is penalties and interest.

Re: New Thread **OPEN THIS ONE** (Ignore the Last One!!)

From: Emily Farris
To: Jan Scott
Subject: Re: Quick copywriting project?
Date: Monday, September 19, 2022, 6:33 PM

Hi, Jan. Great to hear from you! I'd be happy to write the copy for this. Looks pretty simple. It will probably only take me an hour or two. I know you said you don't need it until early next month, but I might just knock it out tonight since I'm going to be pretty busy with another project later this week. I'll send over a first draft sometime tomorrow morning, if not sooner.

Thanks,
Emily

From: Emily Farris
To: Jan Scott
Subject: Re: Re: Quick copywriting project?
Date: Monday, September 19, 2022, 6:47 PM

Hi, Jan. One quick question—and I'm sorry, I should have clarified this before promising you I'd deliver in the morning—but I'm looking at this outline you sent and I'm not entirely sure which product page you want me to link to and that will determine some of the copy for this (and you know how I like to highlight those details!). But I'll get started either way and if I don't hear back from you tonight, I can finish it up really quickly in the morning. Like I said, the whole thing should only take a couple hours max.

Thanks!

From: Emily Farris
To: Jan Scott
Subject: Re: Re: Re: Quick copywriting project?
Date: Monday, September 19, 2022, 7:12 PM

Okay, last email for tonight (I hope!). So I started to write this and I realized that this entire campaign would work so much better if you could create a new landing page and combine a few different elements from the rest of your site. Is there any chance your web designer or IT person could make that happen this week? I'd be happy to mock up what I'm thinking and send it over. I don't think it would be much of a heavy lift—really just setting up a new URL and dropping some photos and products that already exist onto it. Let me know!

———————

From: Emily Farris
To: Jan Scott
Subject: Re: Re: Re: Re: Quick copywriting project?
Date: Monday, September 19, 2022, 7:49 PM

Getting the sense you're probably not on email tonight. Good for you! I wish I could tear myself away from mine sometimes.

Anyway, whenever you do log on, if you just want to give me your web designer's contact info, I can reach out. Probably easier if I just explain what I'm thinking directly to the person who will be building it. (But I'm still totally happy to make that mockup if you think that's better?)

I'll try not to respond (again, ha!) until I hear back.

Thanks!!

———————

From: Emily Farris
To: Jan Scott
Subject: Re: Re: Re: Re: Re: Quick copywriting project?
Date: Monday, September 19, 2022, 9:33 PM

> Actually . . . any chance you could shoot over the login to your website? I thought I had it in my email but now I can't find it.

————————

From: Emily Farris
To: Jan Scott
Subject: Re: Re: Re: Re: Re: Re: Quick copywriting project?
Date: Monday, September 19, 2022, 9:34 PM

> Ope! Never mind! Found it right after I hit Send. Of corse!

————————

From: Emily Farris
To: Jan Scott
Subject: Re: Re: Re: Re: Re: Re: Re: Quick copywriting project?
Date: Monday, September 19, 2022, 9:34 PM

> *Of COURSE. Because of COURSE I know how to spell "course." It's late. And, you know, fat fingers!!!

———————————

From: Emily Farris
To: Jan Scott
Subject: Re: Re: Re: Re: Re: Re: Re: Re: Quick copywriting project?
Date: Monday, September 19, 2022, 10:55 PM

> Okay, I haven't heard back from you yet and I hope you don't mind but I'm going to build a very basic page on your website so you can see what I mean. I won't make it live or anything, but it's just as easy for me to make a mockup on the backend as it is for me to do it in an actual design program (plus, I know all of your assets are already in there). If you like it and your web designer wants to go in and tweak it and make it live, it will be super quick. And if you don't, no worries!
>
> Thanks so much!!

———————————

From: Emily Farris
To: Jan Scott
Subject: Re: Re: Re: Re: Re: Re: Re: Re: Re: Quick copywriting project?
Date: Tuesday, September 20, 2022, 2:27 AM

> Any chance you know the Pantone color for your logo off the top of your head??
>
> Thanks!

———————

From: Emily Farris
To: Jan Scott
Subject: Re: Re: Re: Re: Re: Re: Re: Re: Re: Re: Quick copywriting project?
Date: Tuesday, September 20, 2022, 3:19 AM

NM! Figured it out! Ha!

———————

From: Emily Farris
To: Jan Scott
Subject: New Thread **OPEN THIS ONE**
Date: Tuesday, September 20, 2022, 6:13 AM

Hi, Jan. Starting a new thread. You can just ignore everything I sent in that last thread or delete it entirely. I had a few questions but I ended up answering them myself. Anyway, here's the gist:

So, I know you only wanted, like, three paragraphs on the new offerings, but I wasn't sure which page this copy was supposed to link to and I realized that I could make it so much more persuasive if it was going to link to something that had elements from both. I know how web designers sometimes want six weeks' lead time—even on something so simple as a basic landing page—so since I still

had your website login credentials from when
you had me input copy last year, I just went ahead
and built you a new landing/splash page for this
campaign. I didn't know you had a new content
management system and I was honestly a little
lost when I logged in last night, but now I feel like
I could teach a class about it, so let me know if you
ever need a quick update!!

Anyway, the new page is live, but it's not linked
anywhere, so nobody will be able to find it until
you link to it from another page. You can see it
here. And if you like it and want me to link it from
the main page or create a menu item, I know how to
do that now, too!

I've also attached three different versions of the
copy you requested (and you can find the Google
Drive folder here), so you can choose which one
you like best. And if you prefer some elements
from all of them, just let me know what you like/
don't like and I can make it all work in the second
draft.

Thanks so much!
Emily

———————————

From: Emily Farris
To: Jan Scott
Subject: Re: New Thread **OPEN THIS ONE**
Date: Tuesday, September 20, 2022, 6:15 AM

Oh and PS: I know I gave you an estimate of an hour or two, so I'll still only invoice you for two hours. Don't worry about that!!!

Thanks!!
Emily

You Don't Want
to Be in Love,
You Want to Be
in Love in a Movie

U p until my wedding weekend, when I told him to *just give it up already*, my dad jokingly referred to Kyle as "The Online Predator."

The predator thing was uncalled for, and we actually met in person, but to be otherwise fair to my dad, I had met a *lot* of men on the internet. Save for my two most serious relationships, nearly all the guys I'd dated were connections from matchmaking websites. And, yes, I said websites because I was what you'd call an early adopter of online dating and there was no app for that (or for anything) yet.

I created my first dating profile in 1999. I was seventeen, but thanks to my platinum blonde pixie cut and tragically thick eyeliner, I could have passed for forty in the right lighting. My beatnik-inspired black turtleneck and cropped men's slacks (thrifted and hand-stitched, of course) weren't helping the situation, but at the time, I felt edgy and sophisticated. I was fully aware that my particular aesthetic didn't appeal to teenage boys in Independence, Missouri, but I was mostly fine with it because I didn't want a boy, anyway. I wanted a *man* (though not one as old as the high school janitor, who according to multiple sources, was quite taken by my age-ambiguous vibe).

The problem was that I couldn't seem to find any suitable suitors within Ford Probe–driving distance—at least not IRL. Occasionally, I lusted after slightly older friends of friends who also seemed like they didn't really belong in our methy Midwest town. But they all either had girlfriends or weren't interested in me. Usually both.

Still, I was not without hope. Because Y2K was mere months away, I was uber-connected to my friends thanks to a Nokia 3210 I couldn't afford but *had* to have, and America was very much online. And since I was one of the sixteen million subscribers paying for AOL at the time, I had free access to Love@AOL—a primitive personals section built right into the internet service provider's portal.

Meeting people on the internet wasn't scary or weird. My dad was a computer programmer, and to this day, my favorite Geriatric Millennial calling card is that before I got my first period, I was on the internet in DOS mode—the Microsoft operating system before Windows that was as visually appealing as a calculator's display.

Sure, my early internet experience mostly involved me standing off to the side of my dad's giant particle board desk, my mind completely blown by the fact that he was TALKING

TO PEOPLE THROUGH THE COMPUTER. But I was there, dammit—and as I recall, Dave Farris even allowed me a few of my own short, supervised chats with total strangers who must have been sitting at equally giant IBMs elsewhere in the world.

By the late nineties, talking to people online was old hat. I'd had mostly unfettered access to a slightly more-modern computer and had already spent an unhealthy amount of time in both AOL and Yahoo! chat rooms. Because it was *the nineteen hundreds*, it was still nearly impossible to load a picture of oneself onto a hard drive, so other than our random screen names (emmydawg) and A/S/L (16/F/MO), we could be judged only by our words.

On the internet, with witty banter as the primary measure of attractiveness, I got to be the hottest girl in the room. Socializing through the computer also allowed me the luxury of editing myself. Instead of blurting out something embarrassing, then obsessing over it for the rest of my life, my insecure, perfectionist brain had the time and space to craft sentences that toed the line of edgy and socially acceptable. If I wanted to, I could tweak my replies thirty-seven times before hitting Send.

I was rightfully skeptical of most of the people I chatted with, and the one time I agreed to meet someone in person, I was safe about it. I persuaded my friend Leslie and her boyfriend to join me on a three-hour road trip to see a guy I'd met in a Yahoo! room dedicated to contemporary country music. When describing to him what I looked like, I said, "People always tell me I look like the lead singer of The [Dixie] Chicks."

He made a joke about her being "the fat one," which should have been the end of all that. Instead, I starved myself for three days ahead of our departure and, the morning of, squeezed into my tightest, strongest shapewear and doubled up on padded bras in an attempt to make the rest of my body look smaller. Terrible decisions all around. Especially because after the predictably short "date," my travel companions and I ended up drinking something strawberry-flavored in a cheap motel room and let's just say that having to ask my friend's boyfriend to peel me out of a vomit-soaked girdle—while unsuccessfully trying to conceal the fact that I was wearing two whole bras—was not my proudest moment.

A few months later, when I was alerted to the existence of Love@AOL by a friend of a friend who may or may not have been addicted to meth and who was unapologetically using the service to find casual sex, I somehow decided it was exactly what I needed to meet a respectable young man.

After a long series of bleeps, bloops, static, and screeching that indicated I was establishing a dial-up connection via landline—followed by the iconic "You've got mail" alert—all I had to do was type "Love@AOL" into the search bar to be transported into a cyber world of romantic possibility. As I waited tens of seconds for the page to load, the adrenaline of anticipation coursed through me. In my head, every sign-on was another opportunity to meet all the new smart, attractive men who'd joined Love@AOL since my last sign-on six hours earlier.

In the real world, or at least my virtual corner of it, things played out differently. The dudes within my sixty-mile search radius came across as shadier and sleazier than the ones who frequented the chat rooms. The seemingly earnest ones were either way too nerdy (even for me) or way too old to be trying to get a date with a seventeen-year-old who may or may not have adjusted her birth month to use Love@AOL (and maybe also get a credit card).

I had yet to go on a single date, but already the cycle of hope and disappointment was an emotional roller coaster—and I couldn't get off. Save for my one true video game love, Tetris, I never got into gaming. But I imagine the dopamine rush I got from logging on to a personals site was similar to the excitement a gamer feels when picking up a controller. I was on a mission, and in order to level up and claim victory, I first had to battle my way through a barrage of obstacles and bad guys.

In the middle of my senior year, I decided I was going to move to New York City after graduation and it occurred to me that I could update my /L to get a head start on dating there. Changing my zip code opened the door to a whole new cyber world. Yes, the dudes were still generally nerdy or sleazy, but those qualities exist on a spectrum, and these guys were all over it. Plus, they were sophisticated nerds and sleazeballs. And there were so many of them!

My first-ever *official* internet date happened about three weeks after I arrived. I was barely eighteen and had barely settled into my probably illegal basement studio apartment in Brooklyn, but I'd made getting a landline my priority so I could connect my gargantuan eMachine to the World Wide Web. The lucky lad was a finance bro in his twenties and we were going to meet up in Midtown on a Saturday afternoon. Our plan was to go to the top of the Empire State Building—his idea so I could get the touristy stuff out of the way early—then see where things went from there. I didn't really care about the touristy stuff, but I'd seen *Sleepless in Seattle* enough times to believe I was picking up on some subtext.

As we waited in line to get our tickets, I learned that New Yorkers call the act of waiting in a line waiting *on* line and that this New Yorker's favorite topic of conversation was how much money he supposedly had. He never so much as dropped a ballpark, but it was "a lot." Probably because he still lived in his parents' basement in Queens. And by the time we'd reached the sun-drenched observation deck, a cool basement sounded pretty damn nice. I hate the sun any old day, but it was late July and I was still rocking that head-to-toe black. Once we made it back to street level, he talked as we walked what seemed like the entire length of the island even though my unseasonable outfit included black leather high-heeled boots. Money Bags either didn't notice or didn't care that I was uncomfortable, and after we stopped at a halal cart for water and he bought a bottle for himself but didn't offer to buy me one, I told him I had a headache and split.

My trip to the top of the Empire State Building had been nothing like *Sleepless in Seattle*. But instead of letting myself feel bad about my bad date—or about myself—I boiled water for ramen and fired up the old eMachine to sign back in to Love@ AOL. In a matter of days, I had set up another date.

Spencer was getting his PhD in astronomy at Columbia University and we planned to meet at a Starbucks on the Upper

East Side. "I'll be wearing a green shirt," he wrote the night before our planned meetup. "I can't wait to meet you."

Following an hour-and-a-half commute, I grabbed a table by the window and nervously fixed my lipstick. As I looked up from my tiny mirror, I caught a glimpse of someone I can only describe as a *dorkier* Napoleon Dynamite tromping toward the entrance, hunched over under the weight of a heavy backpack. He was wearing a sweat-drenched, sage-green polo shirt.

Oh, God. Oh, God. Oh, God. Please don't let that be him, I thought. *Please don't let that be him. Please don't let that be him.*

Donny Dorko was headed straight for me, so I looked down and started to dig through my purse—as if doing so might make me fade into the floor or just evaporate.

"Emily?" he asked.

It briefly crossed my mind to say I wasn't Emily. But when you have spiky platinum blonde hair, bright red lips, and your entire wardrobe is shades of black—and you use all of these details to describe yourself to your potential date—faking your identity isn't exactly an option.

"I'm Spencer," he said as he peeled off his sweaty backpack and helped himself to a seat. Before I could say a thing, he held out his clammy hand to grab mine.

"What . . . are you doing?" I asked.

"I'm reading your palm," he said. "To see if we're compatible."

Sadly, this remains one of the great mysteries of my life, because as Spencer caressed my heart line, I blurted out that

I'd suddenly been hit with period cramps and that I had to go home "before things got gruesome." My period was still weeks away, but I knew it was the one condition no man would ever question.

My online dating journey was not off to a great start. And possessing that knowledge did little to deter me. In fact, I saw it as a challenge. I reasoned that if I—a *perfectly normal*, not-at-all-desperate person—was dating online, there had to be others out there, too. I just had to keep looking, keep clicking, keep going out on dates, and eventually I'd find the right guy.

In those early days, it was mostly all fun and games. I could handle the disappointment that inevitably came after spending days or weeks getting to know someone only to lack any chemistry upon meeting in the flesh—as long as I could go home, get online, and find someone new. It was kind of like *Groundhog Day*, but with a different date each time (*Groundhog Date?*). After a while, though, I started to feel like I'd reached the end of the available age-appropriate men in the Tri-state area, so I took a break from browsing profiles and started obsessively searching for a new apartment instead.

Taking a break proved to be a good thing because in the spring of 2003, with my twenty-first birthday quickly approaching, I logged back on and clicked my way to Damian.

By this point, Love@AOL was a distant memory and I'd moved on to edgier sites with better design and more intriguing men. Online dating was becoming somewhat less stigmatized, too, so the pool of potential matches seemed to grow bigger by the day. And—finally!—nearly every profile had at least one grainy, strategically cropped photo.

On my low-resolution screen, Damian was perfect. He was super smart, loved to cook, and *taught music to deaf children*. He was cute, too. In person I found him just as handsome—and quiet in a broody, Dawson Leery kind of way. He was also captivated by my every word. As hard as I tried to find something wrong with him, I couldn't, and I left our first date completely smitten. Yet for reasons I could not articulate, by our eighth date, I still could not talk myself into wanting to have sex with him. No matter how much cheap wine I drank.

"What's wrong with me?" I asked Jo over the phone one morning after Damian had departed yet another sexless sleepover. I was wearing bootcut yoga pants—a detail I remember only because I made sure to put them on as a sort of spandex chastity belt before crawling into bed. "Is he too nice? Am I judging him more harshly because I met him on the internet? Am I just broken?" We agreed that all three things were probably true, and that the kindest thing to do was to end it sooner than later. I also made her tell me it was okay to break up over email since we'd met online.

It took me more than an hour to write what should have been a simple "You're great but this isn't working for me" because I kept overexplaining myself and then editing it way down and starting over (the blessing and curse of communicating online). At some point, I forced myself to hit Send, but instead of feeling relieved, my dread intensified. *When will he read it? How will I know when he does? Will he reply? What will he say? Is he going to hate me?*

To distract myself, I got back to clicking through my possible connections.

With the advent of online images, it didn't take me long to get really good—and really quick—at narrowing down my choices based solely on their profile pictures. I'd long sworn off finance bros and thus decided anyone wearing a suit was far too conventional. But they also had to be wearing a shirt of *some* kind; glistening pecs simply didn't do it for me. Frosted tips were out, too, as was anyone wearing visible cargo shorts, flip-flops, or a goatee. Another girl in your profile pic? Pass. A gun? Fuck right off. I scrolled extra fast past anyone with a Confederate flag in the background, and in the context of a dating profile, even the presence of Old Glory gave off too many Republican vibes for my comfort.

But I'm not a monster; I didn't judge these men on looks alone. I was also an incredibly harsh critic of their words. I wanted wit, I wanted humor, I wanted banter—and I wanted it all to be completely devoid of typos and grammatical errors. In 2005, I penned a post on my personal blog complaining about dudes who didn't bother to use spell-check before sending me a message. "Even worse," I wrote, complaining about internet shorthand, "are the guys who are too lazy to spell out words like *you* and *you're*."

So I had standards. And sure, they were much, much higher than the standards I had for men I met out in the wild. But wasn't filtering out what I *didn't* want the whole point of using technology to find a mate? Without the benefit of chemistry, I had to rely on search criteria, and to me, it was just like buying a plane ticket online: I could set some parameters, be presented with a curated list of nonstop flights, then decide if I wanted to get to LaGuardia at the ass crack of dawn or shell out an extra fifty bucks for the window seat. Plus, was it really too much to ask that Al Gore's internet give me a man with a face like Lenny Kravitz and a vocabulary like Chuck Klosterman?

Duh, yes. I—an overweight, socially awkward, broke no-name writer—was clearly asking for too much. So I cast a wider net with a more open mind and tried to be less of an asshole about spelling. Sometimes I'd get frustrated with the options on one network and switch to another. Other times, I'd meet a guy the old-fashioned way—at a bar or a party, or through a friend. When that happened, I'd deactivate my profile for a few weeks, months, or, once, nearly two years. As soon as one thing ended, I went back online to look for a replacement.

At one point, when I was blogging professionally for the edgy, sex-positive culture site Nerve.com (RIP), I received a promotional thirty-day subscription to Jdate, a service for Jewish singles. I wasn't trying to take up space in a place that wasn't for me, but I was also curious to check it out "for work." In the spirit of full transparency, I made my screen name ShiksaInterloper. My honesty was rewarded with exactly zero Jdates, but just browsing the profiles of people who willingly paid money to use a dating website did inspire me to sign up for free trials of a couple more premium sites.

Save for my interloping, I was running a high-volume operation that resulted in lots of dates. And as people spent more time on their computers, things happened more quickly. I could initiate a message with a guy on a Tuesday and have plans to meet at the dive bar around the corner on Wednesday or Thursday. It was thrilling. It was also completely nerve-wracking.

I wanted the witty banter, to be adored for my words and clever comebacks, to flirt without having to wash my hair or worry about whether the guy across the table thought I was fat. (I always made sure to include a full-body photo to make very clear that I wasn't a size 4, but this was all happening in heroin-chic Brooklyn at the height of skinny celebrities getting publicly fat shamed, and I was determined to avoid my own version of that humiliation.)

On the other hand, I didn't want to waste my time messaging with someone if we weren't going to hit it off in person, so after a few good exchanges, I usually wrote something like: "Well, this is fun, but we're either going to click or not, so why don't we just get it out of the way and meet for a quick drink tomorrow?"

If a first date went poorly—which was most often the case—I rarely devoted any time to introspection. I wasn't questioning whether I'd come across as too eager or too awkward or too aloof or too drunk. (By then I'd realized it was easier to carry on a real-life conversation with a stranger from the internet if whiskey was involved.) If anything, I wholeheartedly believed that my thick thighs, squishy stomach, and comparatively small breasts were the only impediments to me finding love. But I rarely let myself worry about that, because (1) it was depressing as fuck, and (2) the internet was so full of people there had to be one who would love me just the way I was.

But is love what I wanted? Back then, I would have told you, absolutely, yes. And I *did* want someone to love me—or at the very least, be really, really ridiculously attracted to me. I even had a very clear idea of *who* I wanted that someone to be.

But beyond fantasies of sharing a big one-bedroom apartment and having lots of sex, I hadn't actually considered what I might do with the kind of love I thought I wanted.

Ten years after I made my first profile on Love@AOL, technology had improved, public perception of online dating had improved, and the pool of available men had improved. In many ways, I'd improved, too. No, I didn't have my financial shit together, but I was wiser, more sophisticated, fairly accomplished in my career, and without a doubt, my personal style had taken a turn for the better. But over and over again, I let myself get so carried away by the thrill of what *could* be that I failed to do any of the work required to become a person capable of sustaining a healthy relationship. Ninety percent of the time, I could barely make it past a first date—and when I did somehow end up with a serious boyfriend, I was always so eager to move on to the next stage that I couldn't enjoy what I had.

By the end of 2009, I was over it. Eleven months earlier I'd (somewhat impulsively) moved to Kansas City for a big, cheap apartment. My main motivation was having all the rooms all to myself, but it wasn't lost on me that, in addition to my standard of living, my love life might improve, too.

For years, I had blamed New York for my dating woes, yet here I was, nearly a year into living in a new city, waking up after another dead-end date with another dizzying hangover. The setting was new, and (as always) the guy was new, but I was the same old me, doing the same old shit: following the dopamine, freaking out about what could go wrong when it was about to get real, drinking too much to calm my nerves, and blowing any chance of cultivating an actual connection with anyone.

I needed a break. From drinking. From dating. From all of it. So, like nearly every other decision I've made, I decided right then and there that I was going to get off of the hamster wheel, at least for a while.

On New Year's Eve, I had some friends over to help empty my measly bar, and with my last drink (for a while, anyway) in my hand, I ceremoniously deleted my OkCupid profile. I had every intention of creating a new one, but I never got around to it because, seventeen days later, I was at a concert and had the world's shortest conversation with the dude standing behind me. Two years after that, we got married.

I'd be lying if I said I didn't miss online dating—even if what I really long for is the sense of possibility that accompanied it. Now I just have to find other ways to get my dopamine. Social media gives me some of that digital banter I crave, and I almost hate to admit that I get just as much of a thrill from browsing vintage rug listings as I once got from looking at profiles. And like those days when I felt like I'd browsed my way through all the single men in New York, I now occasionally get bored seeing all the same inventory from all the same sellers, and I shift from Etsy to eBay and back again. When things seem really stale, I'll seek out those more expensive antique dealer websites. Similarly, I stride into a thrift store—especially one in a new city—with the same zeal and sense of hope I once had walking into a bar on a Saturday night. The difference is that I almost always get lucky when thrifting.

It's amazing what a little self-awareness can do, though more than a decade into marriage, I'm still trying to nail that whole "becoming a person who's capable of sustaining a healthy relationship" thing. Sometimes I subconsciously pick a fight when life seems to be going smoothly for too long, and I pull away and hyperfocus on a project when I feel like I don't have enough breathing room. I can tell I've sent Kyle into a place of fear and that things are on the verge of getting really bad between us when he starts whistling. And because I love my husband—and just as much because the whistling makes my skin crawl—I do my best to fall back into my marriage.

I fail often, but I never would have known about the whistling thing if I had met my husband on a dating site. Because if I'd seen his cargo shorts, I would have scrolled right on by.

Things I've Forgotten and Things I Don't Think I'll Ever Forget

Things I've Forgotten

My own phone number.

Where I put that La Croix I was still drinking.

The answer to my security question.

My best friend's birthday, on more than one occasion.

My own age, from time to time.

Whether or not I took my Vyvanse this morning.

Where I put that day-of-the-week pillbox I bought so I would never have to remember whether or not I took my Vyvanse.

The capital cities of most of the fifty nifty United States.

To eat lunch.

That Kyle bought me food for lunch and put it in the
    front of the fridge so I'd see it.

To eat dinner.

To check in with Kyle about his day even though
    I have a recurring event on my calendar called
    "Check In with Kyle."

Why I stopped taking vitamins. But it probably has
    something to do with that day-of-the-week pillbox I
    forgot I had. I can't really remember.

To file my taxes.

To file an extension on my taxes.

Which one is Michelle Branch and which one is
    Vanessa Carlton.

How I ever managed to get anything done before
    Vyvanse.

My debit card in an ATM machine, more than once,
    and I'm pretty sure I was drunk every time.

That I have a SodaStream. And I don't know why I'm
    holding onto it because I don't think I'll ever stop
    buying La Croix.

To file my expense report at work, resulting in
    multiple $39 late fees paid directly from me to
    American Express.

How to flirt with strangers.

That I was boiling water for pasta.

How to spell *colonel*. But come on: that is not
    phonetic and it makes no damn sense.

That I was warming a pan for grilled cheese.

The happy memories from when I was a kid.

My address when I lived in the East Village.

My ACT score.

Why I used to bother shaving my legs every single day.

What it feels like to not be tired.

The color of my ex-boyfriend's eyes.

To pick up that thing I was supposed to pick up from my neighborhood Buy Nothing group, but I can't remember what the thing was or who I'm supposed to get it from.

My blood type. It's one of the Os, but I can never remember which one.

How many people I've slept with.

The names of all the people I've slept with.

What it's like to sleep with someone who is not my husband.

Where I put my passport.

When I last had a Pap smear.

How often I'm supposed to have a Pap smear.

To make this year's OB-GYN appointment.

To make last year's OB-GYN appointment.

To move my laundry to the dryer.

To schedule my flu shot.

The answer to today's Wordle, which I just solved, like, twenty minutes ago.

How to do math without a calculator.

To pay my gas bill. Seriously, why is that one not on autopay?

To reply to your email even though I marked it as unread so I would remember. But now too much

time has passed and I'd rather just pretend I never
saw it.

Charlie's little fingers and toes and baby noises and
most of the other amazing, adorable things he did
in his first year because he was born three weeks
before the Covid lockdown and I was consumed
with anxiety.

What it feels like to walk into a restaurant without a
reservation.

What it feels like to walk into a bar on a whim and
stay as long as I want.

What it feels like to have autonomy over my time.

Things I Don't Think I'll Ever Forget

All the lyrics to the rap in TLC's "Waterfalls."

The smell of a rotten lemon.

The smell of a rotten potato, which is somehow worse
than the smell of a rotten lemon.

The dance sequence to the carnival music at the
beginning of Janet Jackson's "If" video.

All the words to Lisa Loeb's "Stay."

All the words to "My Mind Is Mine," the official
theme song of the DARE program.

That time my mom cut my bangs and had to take me
to a salon to fix it and the stylist told me to never,
ever let Barb come near me with a pair of scissors
again.

That there are five hundred twenty-five thousand six
hundred minutes in a year.

That everybody told me my anger and fear after the
2016 presidential election was an overreaction.

That my mom and grandma used to tell me, "You're
not fat, you're big boned." (I wasn't either.)

The night I rode a borrowed bike through a light mist
in Amsterdam.

That my AOL Instant Messenger played the first line
of the Foo Fighters' "Everlong" every time one of
my friends signed on.

To order Nespresso pods.

The pain of childbirth (or at least contractions) before
the sweet, sweet relief of an epidural. They say you'll
forget it, but I didn't.

That time I took an Ambien and didn't fall asleep and
I made Kyle take a video of me as proof that I had
four hands.

Scarlett Johansson's haircut in *A Marriage Story*.

816-796-0516, which was the number to my very
own private phone line I got for my thirteenth
birthday. (Shared with apologies to whoever has
that number now.)

That in his 2006 novel *Absurdistan*, the author Gary
Shteyngart called a 150-pound woman "a big girl."

That when I wrote an entertaining column for a
local design magazine, they Photoshopped out my
tattoos so I'd look more wholesome.

To sing "got to be startin' stuffing" every time I start making my buttery sage stuffing the night before Thanksgiving.

All the bad stuff about Michael Jackson every time I hear a Michael Jackson song and it's a real fucking bummer.

Me, Myself, and My Never-Ending Postpartum Anxiety

Before I had kids, I did not consider myself an anxious person. Sure, Childless Emily was always a little extra, and even as a teenager, I never left the house without at least a few basic first-aid supplies, three Chapsticks, and a toothbrush in my purse. But babies? Babies were easy.

I spent a decent chunk of my twenties working as a part-time nanny—in addition to college and my seventeen or so other jobs—and I felt well equipped to handle anything a newborn might try to throw (or spit or shit) at me. Plus, who better to be up all night with a gassy infant than a woman who already had an erratic sleep schedule? I wasn't afraid of losing my grip on slippery baby skin in that first kitchen-sink bath, I wouldn't be grossed out when the umbilical cord stump unceremoniously detached from the blood-crusted belly button (the green light to finally give that inaugural bath), and I knew precisely how to position a tiny body on my shoulder to work out a burp.

My home was ready, too. In the weeks before Teddy's arrival, I—a person who lives out of laundry baskets—washed and organized a year's worth of cartoonishly small onesies and little pants with adorable designs like hedgehogs and smiling evergreen trees. I spent months designing the perfect nursery with collected pieces that were decidedly not babyish. In fact, the most infantile thing in the room was the crib, empty except for a firm mattress and fitted sheet for safe sleep, of course. For weeks I researched gear for our registry, which included a changing pad that didn't require a cover and was easy to wipe down when it inevitably got pooped and peed on, as well as the safest infant seat on the market at the time.

When people asked if I was going to breastfeed, I snapped back, "I'm going to try and if I can't, I'm not going to feel bad about it," though I later wished I'd just told them it was none of their damn business. When they asked if we'd picked a name, I smugly announced, "Yes, and we're not telling anyone until after he's born." When they asked if I was ready—in the way people do that's more of a warning than an actual question—I hoped they could hear the annoyance in my voice when I said, "I've never been more prepared for anything in my whole life." Because on paper, it was true.

What I was not at all prepared for, however, was what having a baby would do to my brain.

To be fair to the perfectly wonderful former baby in question, it wasn't the act of birthing him that fucked me up (though an infuriatingly long labor followed by an emergency C-section is its own special kind of fuckery). Rather, it was everything that happened in the days after.

The first kink in my Cool Mom plan was extreme sleep deprivation. I knew there would be some sleepless nights, but I did not anticipate being awake for five straight days. Never have I ever been more exhausted than I was after laboring for twenty-six hours, then trying to push a giant baby out of my comparatively small vagina for an additional four hours, only to have it end with an abdominal surgery *for which I was to remain awake.* As soon as I was wheeled out of the operating room, there was a baby on my boob. Well, I tried to put a baby on my boob, but my once-flat nipples were having none of it. My doula taught me how to squeeze my breast into what she called a hamburger, and it helped a little, but we struggled with feeding throughout our stay in the mother–baby unit. Being calm and relaxed surely would have helped, but because I'd had a C-section, nurses came into my room to check my stitches and stats every twenty minutes, which left very little time for rest—especially since different nurses were coming to check on the baby every thirty minutes. (You'd think, as women in STEM, they could have coordinated that better.) Every few hours, the lactation consultant on duty would pop in to check on Teddy's latch, too. When I asked a night nurse if she'd take him for a while so I could sleep, I was told we needed to stay together for bonding and nursing.

Christmas Day we were finally allowed to go home, and with Kyle behind the wheel, I buckled myself into the back seat. We both realized that we'd never noticed quite how reckless other drivers were. I cringed when I recalled that, just three days earlier, on the way to the hospital, I was in so much pain I was screaming at my husband to run red lights and honk his way through crosswalks—pedestrians and their old-ass dogs be damned.

It was such a relief to be home in my own quiet room, far away from the beeping machines and interrupting medical professionals, but I also started to feel anxious and sad. I chalked it up to the lack of sleep and hormones, but the next day I noticed Teddy's diaper had been dry for hours and started to panic. I was putting him on my boob nonstop, but he wasn't peeing. I deduced that nothing was coming out because nothing was going in. I called the nurse line at the local children's hospital and burst into tears when I told the nurse (her name was Kelly, which I'll never forget) what was happening. She helped to calm me down and we made a plan that involved me drinking more water, pumping as much as I could, and in the meantime, offering Teddy a little formula after each nursing session.

On Kelly's advice, we also visited a well-meaning pediatric feeding consultant who encouraged me to keep a detailed breastfeeding log.

I wish she would have just told me to give him formula.

After that appointment, milk production became my only mission in life. I spent hours reading peer-reviewed articles and digging through the comments section of chestfeeding posts on parenting forums. I ate an entire bag of expensive lactation cookies a day and decided I much preferred the lemon flavor to the chalky chocolate chip. I spent a couple hundred bucks on a fancy new pump to replace the mainstream one my insurance had paid for six weeks earlier and then I spent more money to make sure I had the proper flange size for my apparently freakishly small nipples. When I got sick of the lactation cookies, I stuffed my face with artisanal fenugreek breakfast bars because fenugreek is supposed to increase milk production. They gave me more stomach cramps than milk, but I kept eating them and washed them down with coconut water even though it tasted like someone bottled human sweat and sweetened it with high-fructose corn syrup. And for fifteen months, I obsessively opened the Notes app on my phone to jot down the start and stop time of every nursing and pumping session—with yield. But my note-taking didn't end at feeding. I kept a record of day and night sleep, bodily functions (with approximate volume as well as color and texture), and each smile, gurgle, bath, grandparent visit, grocery store outing, and anything else his little body did—and whatever my body did in response.

It went on like this until I decided I wanted to be done breastfeeding. Which happened on Wednesday, April 5, 2017—which I know because of my log.

With the stress of feeding a human from my own body behind me, there was still plenty to worry about. When I finally let someone else put Teddy to bed—a task that was exclusively mine for the first year of his life—I left annoyingly detailed instructions about his bedtime routine. Single-spaced in eleven-point font, my how-to guide took up a whole letter-size sheet of paper. And since there was no chance I would ever trust another human to install a car seat, I refused to show anyone else how to do it. I chastised Kyle for not cutting grapes into small enough pieces and for skipping sunscreen (mineral formulations only) when they went to the park. Out in public, it took everything I had to not gently "educate" other parents when they didn't have their kids properly positioned in a baby carrier or had the car seat chest clip in the wrong place. Then I'd worry about those kids getting hurt and wonder whether or not I did the right thing by keeping my mouth shut.

When I got diagnosed with ADHD, Teddy was two and already deep into what would be a years-long obsession with Spider-Man. I had barely started to realize that I might have been dealing with postpartum anxiety and was forced to re-examine everything through the lens of neurodivergence. What if I'd just been hyperfocused on my worst fears? Or had my hormones merely amplified my already obsessive tendencies? And is any of that really so different from clinical postpartum anxiety?

Two years later, when I got pregnant with Charlie, I focused a smidge less on the perfect nursery and a lot more on my own mental health (though I focused on the nursery, too). Together, my OB, my psychiatrist, and I made a plan for my medica-tion. Kyle and I made a plan to prioritize my sleep from the very beginning and to supplement with formula—and without guilt—if I had milk production issues again. We also decided that, once I was off pain meds and out of adult diapers, I would find a reason to leave the house alone at least once a week, even if just for an hour.

Postpartum Round Two was shaping up to be a breeze. My scheduled C-section felt like a spa day compared to my last stint in Labor and Delivery and I didn't have to use any of the formula samples I'd packed in my hospital bag because my milk came quickly and easily. The doctor running the show discharged us a day early because Charlie and I were both doing so well, and once we were home, we all took turns sleeping. Two weeks in, I told Kyle I was ready to get a babysitter and have a forty-five-minute cocktail date at an actual bar. Most shockingly, I was looking forward to having sex—an activity I avoided for nearly a year after Teddy was born.

I hardly recognized this cool, calm, collected new mom, but I was loving every minute of having a newborn without all-consuming anxiety.

And then the world shut down.

I'd been pretty closely following what was happening in China and Italy, but Cool, Calm, Collected Emily naively assumed that, like so many of the global viral scares that had dominated the headlines in my lifetime, it wouldn't be so bad in the United States. (It must have temporarily slipped my mind that I'd been warning everyone who would listen that Trump was going to get us all killed.)

Overnight, I went from blissfully soaking up baby snuggles to ordering supplies for DIY bleach wipes and stalking the internet for just one goddamned bottle of Children's Tylenol. I snapped at Teddy for breathing too close to Charlie and made Kyle wear his lawn-mowing shoes to the store so as not to track in any virus on his regular sneakers. I also disinfected the groceries he bought, but only a few times.

A week after Kyle was sent home from his brewery job, he was officially furloughed. Teddy's preschool shut down indefinitely. I felt I had no choice but to prematurely end my measly, self-imposed maternity leave, so I started hustling for writing and design work. In between small marketing projects and epic cluster feeds, I tried to stay on top of the mess that magically appears when a preschooler is suddenly home all the time. But I couldn't stay on top of it, and there was no way and no*where* to get away from the noise or the nursing newborn. And no matter how hard I tried, I couldn't manage to keep the floor clear enough to run the robot vacuum, so my house quickly went from "Instagram-worthy if you catch it at the right angle" to an aesthetic that more closely resembled "condemned day care but with cute rugs and half-dead plants." At one point, I worried I'd developed some sort of vaginal infection and beat myself up for skipping my six-week postpartum checkup. I was both relieved and disgusted when I finally figured out that the smell was not wafting out of my crotch but coming from the toilet—which hadn't been cleaned since before Charlie was born and was getting more use than ever before.

I was overstimulated and overwhelmed with everything happening in my house and also grappling with the idea that the only thing to *do* about the pandemic in those first few months was to do nothing at all. Obviously, I was incredibly grateful for the ability to keep my family isolated—and very aware that staying home was a huge privilege—but my brain was better suited for slaying supervillains than it was for sheltering in place.

Long before I knew I was neurodivergent or that thinking on my feet was an ADHD superpower, I bragged about being the kind of person you want to have around in the apocalypse. I've always been good in emergencies and I'm industrious like a modern-day MacGyver. Though I have not been given the chance to prove my Lady MacGyver theory under the life-threatening circumstances the prime-time protagonist faced, I have performed the Heimlich maneuver on a choking toddler, fixed the tail lights on my old Volvo in the grocery store parking lot, rescued an emaciated puppy from oncoming traffic, and once fashioned a pour-over coffee maker from a dish towel and a mesh sieve because not having caffeine in the morning absolutely counts as an emergency. Also, dystopian fiction happens to be my favorite literary genre, so I like to pretend I know a thing or two about fighting off the walking dead (though my skills are probably on par with Teddy's ability to stop a bad guy by shooting webs at him).

But I wasn't a zombie slayer or even a front-line worker; I was a freelance writer on maternity leave and my one job was to do the same safe thing in the same safe place day after day after day after day. Like a high-energy dog that doesn't get enough exercise, I became anxious and agitated.

The feeling was nothing new; I'd simply traded postpartum anxiety for pandemic anxiety.

Parenting had made my life more hectic in all the ways I expected, but it also forced me into an uncomfortable state of slow motion. With a helpless human under my care and often attached to my boob, I was forced to sit—sometimes for hours on end—with my own thoughts. Instead of giving my brain the dopamine it craved by picking up a paintbrush or tearing down a wall, my mind raced with what-ifs and worst-case scenarios. In the early months of lockdown, that also meant nonstop doomscrolling and reading everything I could find on infants and Covid (which wasn't much).

I knew obsessively reading the news wasn't good for me, but just like with Teddy's feeding log, it was a way for me to feel at least a little bit in control. Plus, in a twisted way, my anxiety was feeding the dopamine monster, and at the very least, it was enough to keep me from falling asleep and smothering my baby—one of my many fears with both boys.

As we approached the one-year mark of what was supposed to be our three-week lockdown, we discovered Charlie had a pretty severe nut allergy.

"Will we ever not be anxious?" I texted my friend Gina, whose anxiety seems to rival mine at times. "Or is this just what life as a parent is like now?"

Kyle and I were cautiously optimistic when vaccines became available and I sobbed when I got my first shot. Not because it hurt but because I hoped it was the beginning of a return to normal and the end of my second bout of anxiety after having a baby—whether it was technically postpartum anxiety or not.

As I write this, it's been 953 days since we were first told to shelter in place. The world hasn't really gotten better, but Charlie's nut allergy has, thanks to science delivered to us in the form of a pediatric allergist who introduced the idea of oral immunotherapy (basically microdosing with allergens under close observation). We even survived Covid, which Charlie picked up from his (vaccinated) day care teacher eleven days before the FDA approved shots for kids younger than five. Months later, Kyle continues to have some long Covid symptoms, but we keep reminding ourselves that it's nowhere near as bad as it could have been.

As for my anxiety, I don't think it will ever fully go away because I think it *is* just what life as a parent is like now.

Being busy with work gives me less time to think about the worst things that could happen, but, of course, I still worry. About idiots texting and driving while my family is out on the road. About the algorithm feeding Teddy white supremacist propaganda when he finally figures out he can get onto You-Tube without adult supervision. About school shootings. About day care shootings, too, because that's probably next, right?

I have yet to allow anyone else to install a car seat and I get panicky if Kyle forgets to grab Charlie's backpack when they go to the grocery store because that bag is where we keep the EpiPen and it's supposed to be with him at all times. I worry about head injuries when they're at the playground and brain-eating amoebas if one of them gets a little bathwater up their nose.

Sometimes, when I'm watching them play, I find myself wondering whether Teddy will be able to take care of Charlie if my Zombie-fighting skills aren't as sharp as I thought and Kyle and I don't survive the apocalypse after all. Have I been so protective of them that they'd be the first to fall in a Lord of the Flies scenario? Instead of just crossing the nearly dried-up creek while running for their lives, will Teddy grab his brother's arm and point out that they're not supposed to go into the water without a life jacket? Will Charlie be washed away by rising flash floods because he's not supposed to go up the stairs without an adult?

But there's one thing I don't worry about when it comes to my kids: ADHD.

So far, neither has shown any glaring signs, but they're still pretty young and recent studies have put the heritability around 80 percent, so the odds aren't exactly in their favor.

If it turns out they do have it, they'll be fine. In fact, I think they'll be more than fine. For starters, they're middle-class white males, but more importantly, they're going to have the tools and support I didn't.

My parents did the best they knew how to do, but Kyle and I know better. Instead of a mom who spanks them because they can't settle down at bedtime, my kids have a mom who can help them find ways to calm their minds and bodies. Instead of one day realizing they've never actually met any of their dad's friends and being too afraid to ask why, they have a dad who will teach them how to make small talk and take them on camping trips with other families. And they'll never have to wonder "what's wrong with me?" because they'll be surrounded by adults who know that ADHD isn't a character flaw and that, if properly harnessed, neurodivergence can be a superpower.

At forty, I'm still learning how to harness my own powers, but I work at it every day, because like Spider-Man always says, "With great power comes great responsibility."

A Shed of One's Own

In *A Room of One's Own*, Virginia Woolf famously declared, "A woman must have money and a room of her own if she is to write fiction." I would argue the same is true for women who write nonfiction—and really, for any person who requires extra time and space to hear their own thoughts. Nearly a hundred years since Woolf's pivotal proclamation, this "room" is more important than ever. But it's due for some serious upgrades (and yeah, they're probably gonna be pricey).

For example: If the woman in question has small children and a husband whose telephone voice transcends space, time, and plaster walls older than Woolf's manuscript, this room is ideally detached—though still a walkable distance—from one's primary residence. Soundproofing may also be explored as an alternative or additional option. The space should be free of juvenile toys, dishes that require washing, the stench of urine deposited next to the toilet by school-age boys or full-grown men, and myriad life's daily stressors. Fixtures and amenities could include but not be limited to velvet window dressings, off-white upholstery, and even a miniature icebox for convenient access to chilled seltzer.

If for some reason, the woman were to be imprisoned in
the shared family home with the aforementioned spouse and
offspring for nearly two years, the renovation of a new room—
though preferably the construction of a detached dwelling—
would require the utmost urgency. Should a husband attempt
to override his wife's wishes over financial concerns during this
time, the woman may consciously or subconsciously descend
into a petulant, hostile state. In this case, it is best to keep the
shared home as clean and quiet as possible so as not to cause
serious resentment in the marriage and to maintain a peace-
ful abode for the children. Far better than simply keeping the
peace, however, is clearing a path for the woman to build what
she truly desires: a shed of one's own.

One may be forgiven for lacking the knowledge that a
sacred retreat has been the woman's lifelong objective, but there
is no better time for education than the present. Therefore, it
must be understood that a grown woman who aches for a room
(or detached dwelling) of one's own surely dreamed of secret
gardens and secluded nooks as a youth. With the passing of
years, she may have adorned closets with cushions and textiles
to mimic a private parlor—free from the whims and clatter of
those who often dismissed her frequent need for silence and
privacy. As she progressed into womanhood, it would not be
unlike her to haul the entirety of her worldly belongings (and
perhaps her feline companion) halfway across the country and
settle for unsatisfactory living conditions in pursuit of a pre-
dominantly undisturbed home life.

Now it is the duty of the spouse to understand that this
yearning does not fade with love, marriage, or childbearing. In

fact, he should recognize that such events may cause the woman's longing to intensify tenfold—before taking into account any plague that may require blood relations to self-contain in the home for an extended period.

And should the woman give birth to yet a second son a mere three weeks before the onset of nationwide calamity, and should she be unexpectedly and simultaneously thrust into the role of sole earner by default (though by no fault of the husband), the need for a sanctuary space will become ever more urgent.

So it is imperative that the manufacture of this room (or detached dwelling) become a critical cause for everyone who inhabits the domesticity of origin. Further, all involved parties must put out of mind that the woman is without inheritance and has more than exhausted her meager wages on daily expenditures (with modest allowances for a few of life's little pleasures, of course). Despite her fear of personal financial depression, it is true that in the woman's eyes, this room (or detached dwelling) is more than a matter of bank debt. For without it, she feels she will die.

Color of the Year

D o you understand what I'm trying to tell you?"

"Mmhm," I offered slowly, intentionally, as confirmation that I heard and understood exactly what Kyle was trying to tell me. Even though I didn't really.

He was complaining to me about something I'd done. Maybe it was money I'd spent without telling him. Or maybe he was upset that I'd rushed out earlier when he was trying to have a discussion about dinner. Or was it a bill we needed to pay? Either way, here he was trying to talk to me again. I could see his mouth moving. I could hear noise coming out of it. I caught a few random words. But none of it stuck. Because right behind his head, in the weak 6:00 p.m. April light bleating in from our north-facing windows, I noticed that the pale gray color of the kitchen walls was just too cool, even compared to the silvery white I'd chosen for the adjacent dining room.

When I'd hastily picked the paint at Home Depot two years prior, I should have known better than to put a cool gray in a room with northern exposure, but I didn't know as much about undertones back then. At the time, I was satisfied with calling it "a sort of dove gray," but the way it was illuminated that spring evening, it looked almost purple. And all of a sudden, I hated it.

I decided it had to go. Like, immediately. Because when I was in the kitchen, that almost-purple cool gray was all I could see. I could see it from the living room and dining room, too.

The urge to cover it was as intense as the need to wash off stage makeup the second the curtain closed on a high school theater performance. Or to pick off my entire gel manicure after noticing one tiny chip. And as much as I wanted to be, I was not the type of person who could decide to change a paint color and continue to live with the old one for a few days—let alone a few weeks or months.

Evidently, I wasn't a very trendy person either, because this was happening in 2014 when Pantone—the company that creates and names colors for the entire world—had declared purple its color of the year. Well, Radiant Orchid to be more exact. It was a bright, almost iridescent purple that reminded me of the puffy stick-on earrings I used to wear in the nineties. My kitchen walls were much more muted and subdued than Radiant Orchid, but I still couldn't stand them.

I didn't always hate purple. When I was a kid, purple was my favorite color. I wanted purple sheets, purple clothes, purple My Little Ponies. I don't know why I have such a visceral reaction to it now. Can a color trigger some sort of PTSD from unresolved childhood trauma? Maybe it's that it reminds me too much of that time I threw up an entire bottle of red wine all over a sidewalk—and my brand-new North Face parka—waiting for the N train in Astoria. The reason doesn't matter, though, because once I noticed the purple undertones, I couldn't think about anything else.

This was an unfortunate turn of events, considering I had work to do and a husband demanding my time and attention. Any time, any attention. And I'm sure whatever he was lecturing me about was important, but was it as important as the fact that our kitchen was a total design disaster? To me, in that moment, it was not. Also not important? That I had no time to paint. And no money for paint supplies. Or that I was likely the only person who would notice or care about the cool undertones, maybe ever.

For the next few days, the only thing that mattered—the only thing that would benefit from my time, my money, my attention, and my usually good eye for color—was the kitchen. More specifically, its way-too-cool gray walls.

When I told Kyle what was happening, what *had* to happen, he looked at me like I had just asked for a divorce.

"But don't you see the *purple* in this?" I pleaded, though I already knew what he was going to say.

"No. Absolutely not," he said. "It's the same color as the dining room. And I'm trying to have a real conversation right now."

(The kitchen was an entirely different color than the dining room. Anyone could see it. Well, anyone but Kyle, apparently.)

"I'm trying to have a real conversation, too. About paint colors," I snapped back. "Just because you're color-blind doesn't mean colors aren't a real thing."

I knew this was a sore spot. Kyle prides himself on his eyesight, which he can claim is perfect only because he hasn't had an eye exam since high school. And no matter how many times I've tried to explain to him that 20/20 vision has nothing to do with color comprehension—and that scientific evidence supports the theory men are much more prone to color blindness than women—he takes it as a personal attack. He's not truly color-blind, at least I don't think he is. He's just not incredibly color *discerning*. To Kyle, white paint is white paint is white paint and he certainly can't tell the difference between a cool gray and a warm gray, or even navy blue and charcoal.

What I probably should have said was, *Just because you don't care about subtle differences in color doesn't mean they aren't real.*

Or I could have given him some facts in plain old black and white.

> Perceptually and cognitively, men and women may experience appearance of color differently [and] females can see more shades of colors than males.
> — Nidhi Jaint et al., "Gender Based Alteration in Color Perception"

Instead, I set myself up for a fight.

"Do you even know the difference between warm and cool colors?" I demanded.

That was enough for him to walk away. Surely for a few minutes and hopefully for a couple of hours. Plenty of time for me to make it to the hardware store and back, and maybe start taping off the cabinets and trim.

I wanted to *want* to listen to him, to engage with him. I just had to get this paint situation fixed first. Or maybe at the same time? If Kyle had been interested in painting, too, we could have gone to the store together, made road maps to nowhere with blue masking tape, talked about dinner or bills or whatever he wanted to talk about while we rolled a fresh coat of Crisp Linen White on the walls. But he had no desire to repaint a room with what he believed was an identical color, and he couldn't understand why I did, so this would have to be a solo mission. Yet again.

Like "color blindness," the term "attention deficit hyperactivity disorder" is very misleading. A color-blind person doesn't see the world in grayscale; their brain just interprets certain colors differently from how other people's brains do. And my problem is not that I can't focus or pay enough attention; it's that I focus *too* much once something has commanded my attention. I often focus so intently on an exciting project or task that it keeps me from eating, keeps me from sleeping, and keeps me from getting up to pee even when I feel like my bladder is going to explode. It keeps me from carrying on a simple chat with my husband about meals—or any of the pressing married-people topics he attempts to discuss on a regular basis. So no, I don't have an attention deficit. I just can't always focus on what other people want me to focus on when they want me to focus on it. This makes the already-stressful institution of marriage extra stressful.

Once in a blue moon, the stars align, and my brain and Kyle's brain are focused on the same thing at the same time. When that happens, it gives me hope that our relationship will continue to get better. I know he just wants to feel like I care about him as much as I care about paint colors, the way it must have felt when we were new and he was the subject of my hyper-focus. But I don't.

After ten years of marriage, I no longer get excited when I see he sent a text, and when our legs touch under the dinner table, it (usually) doesn't make my heart race like it used to. And that's exactly how I know that my love for him has grown into something bigger and better and more real than a series of dopamine triggers. Because even without the newness and novelty—and with his beer farts and incessant monitoring of our joint bank account—I still want him. He's not a cool gray I'll paint over in a few years or a pile of decorative baskets I'll shove on some shelf in the garage. Our marriage is my home.

Unfortunately, just like with our physical home, sometimes I neglect my marriage. I can only keep up with maintaining it for so long before my brain gets distracted by something else. And when either goes too long without my attention, things get messy, and when the mess becomes overwhelming, I tend to avoid it, which only makes things worse.

As I write this in 2022, Pantone's Color of the Year is called Very Peri. It's a cutesy name for periwinkle, which is technically a shade of blue, but it's always looked a little purple to me.

Yes, I Have a Body

You didn't really think that I, a woman whose most formative (and by "formative" I mean "emotionally damaging")
years happened in the nineties, could write an entire collection of personal essays without writing one about my body . . .
did you?

I can count on one hand the things that have occupied my
mind nearly nonstop for the last forty years, and unfortunately
my body—and its myriad flaws—is one of them, so here we are.

But today is your lucky day because I am so goddamn sick
of reading essays about how much women hate their bodies.
Yes, even if, like me, patriarchal society has conditioned those
women to loathe their own forms and their missives are a giant
middle finger to the man. Even if, like me, they will never forget and frequently recall that June 1993 *Seventeen* magazine
cover featuring the "normal girl" who didn't look exactly like
Kate Moss and so everyone called her fat. And even if, like me,
they layered two padded bras in high school, and two decades
and two breastfeeding babies later they're still waiting for their
boobs to come in. (Though I imagine that last one is probably
just me?)

I'm not going to write about how fat or skinny I think I am and how I've hyperfocused on my own imperfections because of my ADHD, among other reasons. Or how, when I lived in Brooklyn, my friend Lacey offered to set me up with my musician crush and I told her to let me lose twenty pounds first but I never lost it and the meeting didn't happen. I'm not going to tell you how much I weigh to make me seem more relatable or about all the times I attempted and failed to lose weight and how I've finally accepted my body as is. Because while I'd like to think I have, I haven't—not really.

I did write about the time I saw a hypnotist for weight loss, but I have no desire to revisit the topic—although I can see now that the success probably had more to do with the rush of trying something new and less to do with actual hypnosis. If you're dying to read it, it's easy to find online. As is the piece I wrote about how I gained weight while breastfeeding.

I also have zero desire to recount the times I lost weight when I wasn't trying because those were some of the lowest points in my life—as was the time I took diet pills that turned me into someone who very well could have starred in her own Real Housewives franchise. Nor do I want to go into any more detail than I already have about the months I did my best to believe in the power of Overeaters Anonymous meetings even though it felt all wrong; turns out it was merely another instance of me worrying I was addicted to something when, in reality, my body was just desperate for more dopamine.

I mean no offense to the women who write those essays. Their pieces are an essential part of The Discourse™, and I'm sure writing and publishing their accounts is cathartic. Reading their vulnerable and often familiar stories has certainly made me feel less alone in my self-loathing. In fact, I was supposed to write one of those essays myself, and for months and months and months I tried to do it, but I just can't. I've already wasted four decades (and six hundred words) disliking my body and, God, isn't it fucking boring?

A Fairly
Comprehensive
List of Everyone
I Think Is Mad at Me,
with Notes

Kyle, and I could write a whole book about why and
   I guess I kind of did. Or at least, like, a third of a
   book.

My boss every time we're about to go into our
   standing one-on-one meeting.

My dog, for not walking him enough.

My mom, for being too much like my dad.

My dad, for not being enough like him and probably
   also for being too much like him.

My dad, for writing this book in which I talk about
   S-E-X.

My dad, for writing this book in which I talk about
   having an abortion.

My dad, for having an abortion.

My dad, for having sex outside of a marriage, which resulted in me getting pregnant, which resulted in me having an abortion, which resulted in me writing about having an abortion.

My dad, for a somewhat-accidental rager I threw at his house when I was fifteen, and I know for a fact that reading this sentence will make him even more pissed than anything I wrote about sex or abortions.

My mother-in-law, for writing about my abortion in this book she otherwise would want to tell her church-lady friends to read.

My little sister Jo, for still bossing her around even though we're both grown women with children of our own.

My older sister Heather, for that one thing I said at Christmas that one year.

My brother-in-law David, for making Heather so mad.

Melanie, my best friend since the first grade whose wedding shower I missed when I, her maid of honor, accidentally double-booked myself.

My friend Amanda, for breaking one of her cool vintage glasses with colorful dots when we lived together in Park Slope in 2004. Except I also broke a second one and never told her about it. (Amanda, if you're reading this, I want you to know that I still look for those glasses every time I go thrifting because I am determined to replace them.)

My neighbor, who I stopped inviting over once I
  found out she was an anti-vaxxer.
My second cousin, for still being friends with his
  ex-girlfriend.
That lady I ran into at the grocery store last week who
  apparently I was supposed to know but I have no
  idea who she is or how I'm supposed to know her.
The client whose website I started designing before
  I took my full-time job and started writing this
  book, and thus stopped doing freelance anything. I
  followed up with him many times for information
  and feedback so I could wrap up his project, and
  though he's the one who never got back to me, I'm
  sure he's mad at me for not finishing it.
The Boerum Hill, Brooklyn, coffee cart guy I started
  avoiding in the mornings once I found a brick-and-
  mortar coffee shop I liked better. It was 2006 and I
  still feel bad about it.
That guy who sent me so many Twitter messages I
  just stopped opening them. And, honestly, he can
  be mad at me, because at forty years old, I finally
  realized I don't owe any man my time (unless I'm
  related to or employed by him, I guess).
My mother-in-law's sister who never got a thank-you
  card for the gift she sent after Teddy was born. But
  that's Kyle's side of the family and I don't think
  I should be the only one responsible for sending
  thank-you cards simply because I'm the one with a
  vagina. (And let's not forget that I'm the one who

had to endure ten months of pregnancy, thirty
hours of labor, an emergency C-section, and bloody
nipples.)

Everyone else who never got a thank-you card for the
gifts they sent after Teddy was born. But do I really
need to tell you about my damaged vagina and
bloody nipples again?

Everyone who never got a thank-you card for the
gifts they sent after Charlie was born. (Seriously,
people—please stop giving me gifts if you expect a
thank-you card in return.)

All the people who never got thank-you cards for
anything before I had the broken vagina/bloody
nipple excuse.

My kids, for putting sunscreen on them every
morning, even in the winter. They're gonna thank
me later and I tell them that all the time and they're
probably mad at me for that, too.

The people who bought my social media copywriting
class for the full price of $249 right before I decided
I hated selling things online and put it on eternal
clearance for $69.

The other moms at both my kids' schools, for not
volunteering to help with any class parties. And also
for not inviting any other kids over for playdates.
And also for not RSVPing to any of their kids'
birthday parties until they send a text asking if
we're coming.

The day care treasurer, for always being about a
month behind on my bill. If I could just automate
this shit, it would get paid on time.
The pharmacist, every time I fill my Vyvanse
prescription.
All the people I forgot to include on this list who are
now gonna be super pissed at me for that.

I'll Just Be
Five More Minutes

'll be quick," I say. And I mean it. I believe it. I always do.
There's no way this will take long, whatever it is. I'm generally
pretty fast, sometimes I'm even efficient. And, yeah, I've been
known to cut a few corners. To use a drywall screw to hold
a thing in place when I probably should have used . . . anything but a drywall screw. To skim the manuals or ignore them
altogether because, honestly, instructions usually just slow me
down.

"Promise?" he asks.

"Promise," I say. And I mean it. I believe it. I always do.

So I take it apart. Or remove it from the wall. Or open it
up. If I'm opening it up, it's probably a pipe. And it's not like I
have a plan, but I don't need one because my brain just figures
this shit out as I go. And I'm quick. And sometimes efficient,
remember? Plus, I have drywall screws, for fuck's sake. Drywall
screws are the duct tape of hardware. But I also have duct tape.
Rolls of it. In multiple colors. Though I don't know where any

231

of them are at the moment, so I'll probably buy another roll or two tomorrow.

Anyway, I can't think about that now, because currently I'm focused on getting this thing done swiftly so we won't be late for dinner. Of course, I don't really care if we're late for dinner, but he hates being late and I don't want him to get mad at me. Again. So I just have to focus on finishing this so I have time to shower and get ready and get out the door on time.

I grab the white plastic mixing bowl that's home to some of my favorite hand tools and hardware (and also a tube of orange lipstick and a tampon) and I tug or saw or sand or twist. Then I notice that it's kinda gross back there. Or down there. Or under that thing. And I can't keep going when I could easily take sixty seconds to clean it up.

But getting up would break my flow, so I start with the crusty old sponge that also happens to be in my bowl of goodies. It's a little hard, so I spit on it. It's fine.

God, this is so satisfying, I think as I continue to spit and wipe away layers and years of dust or grime or grease or glue.

"Baaaaabe, what are you doing in there?" he hollers from the other room. Could he hear me spitting? "I thought this was just a quick fix!"

"It was nasty under there! Just cleaning real quick before I finish up," I holler back. I realize this will actually go more quickly if I use functional cleaning supplies, so I force myself up and bolt into the kitchen to grab bleach spray and a scouring pad from under the sink. I know I have dish gloves, but I'm not sure where they are, so I decide I'm willing to temporarily wreck my hands for this cause.

"Everything's fine," I say as I scurry back to my station, for some reason trying to hide the fact that I've now acquired additional tools for this job. "Don't worry!"

I'll just finish up this one little patch of filth, then get back to the task at hand, I think to myself. But every time I try to stop, I can't. Because if I leave one sparkling clean patch next to a filthy patch, I will never, ever stop thinking about it. Ever.

I lift my left wrist to my face. "Siri, set a five-minute timer."

After what feels like maybe forty-five seconds, my watch starts to vibrate and chime. With my right pinky finger—the only available digit that's not covered in bleach—I hit snooze. *Just once,* I tell myself.

I use the tip of one of my drywall screws to pick away at the toughest, tiniest bits of gunk.

"Babe?"

"It's FINE!" I yell back. And I can tell by the tone of my own voice that I'm now annoyed with him though I have no right to be. But I can't very well put the thing back together while it's still nasty back there. And I will be physically and mentally incapable of doing or thinking about anything else—anything at all—until I just get this whole fucking project wrapped up.

"I don't really need to wash my hair today, so we still have plenty of time," I assure him. I do need to wash my hair, especially after all this dirty work, but isn't this why God invented dry shampoo?

It occurs to me this is why he was nervous about me starting this little project in the first place, so I convince myself it's clean enough—though I could totally spend three more hours on this single square foot of surface that no one will see for at least another decade or longer. Probably not until someone buys this old house and guts it and discovers all the wonky repairs I've made, all the holes in the plaster I filled with tampons then covered in joint compound and painted before they were fully dry.

I toss my jumble of supplies—spit-and-bleach-soaked sponges and all—into my screw bowl and get back to tugging or sawing or sanding or twisting. But something cracks. Something's not right. Something didn't go according to my nonexistent plan. But I can fix it. I always do.

"Five more minutes!" I call out, answering him though he didn't ask me anything this time. "I'll just be five more minutes!"

And, still, I believe it. I always do.

The Scenic Route

If we go anywhere in a car together and you ask me to navigate, I will get us hopelessly lost. Yes, even in these modern times with Siri as my wing woman. This isn't because I have a horrible sense of direction (though I do) or because I always seem to overshoot the turns on Google Maps and then blurt out "GO LEFT! GO LEFT! LEFT!" to correct course before poor Siri can reroute us (which I also do) but because I am overly confident in my direction dictation. So confident, in fact, that even if I've gotten us lost every single time we've been on the road together—and even if those times add up to more than ten—you'll still listen to me when I tell you to go left.

With Jo, one such adventure culminated with me accidentally peeing into my brand-new red patent leather shoe at an abandoned rail yard after we impulsively got matching sister tattoos and got extremely turned around on the way to our next stop. On a drive up the West Coast with my friend Ruth, it led to a spontaneous stay in a dreamy yurt on an Oregon beach when I'd somehow navigated us too far beyond any halfway decent motels.

I don't necessarily need to be in a car for some variation on this scene to play out, though. Back before we had husbands and ride-sharing apps, I suggested my friend Kristina and I walk to our massage appointments since I'd just gotten a Fitbit and was overly enthusiastic about meeting my daily step goal. We'd joined a cheap "spa" and it was one of the few places in town I could find without the help of AI; there was no question of how to get there. But my reputation for lateness preceded me, so Kristina mapped the route for walking time and very smartly showed up at my house with an extra fifteen minutes to spare.

About forty-three minutes into our otherwise pleasant "forty-five-minute" walk, she stopped in her tracks.

"Wait!" I could hear the anxiety in her voice. "Where are we?"

We both recognized the perfect little suburb with its cottages full of upper-middle-class white people, but it was nowhere near our destination, so I opened the Maps app and rotated my phone a few times to get my bearings.

Somehow, we'd crossed into a whole other state. On foot. Crossing into another state isn't uncommon when you live two blocks from the Missouri–Kansas border, but still.

"Why did you let me walk us across State Line?!" I asked her, genuinely flummoxed.

"Well, you were just so confident when you told us to turn right, I didn't think to question it," she said.

We made it to the spa, albeit late, and only because I flagged down an SUV whose driver looked more like a Mary Kay rep than a serial killer and begged her for a ride. She obliged, and after I told her how I'd gotten us lost, she asked if I was interested in finding Jesus.

Kyle is the only one impervious to my confidence in the car. Thirteen years into our relationship, he knows better than to ask me to navigate, but every once in a while he has no choice. In these instances, he takes what he calls "the George Costanza approach"—a reference to a *Seinfeld* episode titled "The Opposite," in which the socially clumsy, insecure best friend George decides things might go better for him if he just does the complete opposite of what he's always done. It worked for George; after near-constant rejection from various women, he finally scored a date by leading with "My name is George. I'm unemployed and I live with my parents." So now, when I'm in the car with Kyle and I yell, "GO LEFT! GO LEFT," he hears, "My name is Emily. I have zero sense of direction and my mouth is saying 'left,' so you must absolutely go right." And it works. Every goddamned time.

But save for those rare occasions I have to navigate because we're forced to reroute when Kyle is behind the wheel, he knows exactly where he's going. He loves reminding me that he never gets in the car without first having the entire drive mapped out in his head. And no matter how many times he's tried to impart this wisdom upon me—and it's probably been hundreds of times—it has still never once occurred to me to take the time to map out a whole plan (in my head or anywhere else) while I'm scrambling to find my keys so I can rush out the door. It's annoying how perfectly this illustrates the difference between my neurodivergent brain and his neurotypical one.

I come by my shitty sense of direction honestly. When my dad would pick us up for our every-other-weekend visits, the drive was always a little unpredictable. As Dave Farris wended his way from the meth-ridden "suburb" where Jo and I lived with our mom to his apartment in the city, we took in the sights from the back seat. And there were always sights to be seen. Sometimes we got to cruise by old buildings that may or may not have had some sentimental value. Other times, we drove through parks to—I guess—look for deer. Or at deer? More than once, we ended up in one of those hellish developments where every house is beige and every street is somehow also a cul-de-sac so you feel like you'll never be able to find your way out.

I always loved our detours, but Jo found them painfully boring—especially the deer gazing. Part of her problem, I'm sure, had to do with the fact that we were freezing cold half of those weekends because Dad was a chain-smoker back then and kept the window cracked an inch or so—as if a sliver of fresh air could protect his young daughters from the long-term effects of hot boxing Merit Regulars in a Toyota Corolla. I almost always managed to make myself comfortable enough with whatever flannel shirt I found on the floorboard among the discarded newspapers and cigarette cartons and tried to enjoy the view. But even when we shared the dirty shirts like too-small blankets, Jo was far from amused. Whenever she would complain, Dad would inform us that we should appreciate these drives with a line that became his catchphrase in the car: "We're taking the scenic route."

It took me years to figure out that meant he was lost.

To be fair to my dad, I think there was always a foundation of truth to the scenic route story. He certainly knew his way around the greater Kansas City metropolitan area's main thoroughfares—which I know because he detailed for me more than once the numbering conventions for both inter- and *intra*-state highway systems. So I believe that he really did intend to explore a back road or cut over to an old neighborhood from time to time. I also believe that once he got that out of his system, he had no clue how to get back to the highway—which I know because we have the same brain.

On my thirty-sixth birthday, when I told my stepmom I'd been diagnosed with ADHD, her response caught me off guard, though it probably shouldn't have.

"Interesting," she said. "Your dad got diagnosed with that a few years ago."

I wasn't surprised my dad had ADHD—it explained so much—and since my family will do anything to avoid uncomfortable conversations, I guess I also shouldn't have been surprised no one bothered to tell me. But considering that nearly half of all parents with ADHD go on to have neurodivergent kids, it might have been nice for someone to pick up the phone or send an email and say, "Hey, Emily. Your dad just got diagnosed with ADHD. I know, super weird it happened after he was sixty, right? Anyway, it turns out this thing runs in families. And you know how you're always late and we've always joked that you couldn't find your way out of a paper bag to save your life and you're always broke and you took six years to finish college and you timed out of reading comprehension on the GRE even though you're a professional writer and you drink too much and blurt out things you shouldn't? Well . . . maybe you should look into getting checked for this attention brain deficit thing."

Looking in the proverbial rearview mirror, my dad's ADHD is as obvious as mine should have been. Like how he would stay up all night doing who knows what on the computer even in the early nineties when it was likely possible to reach the literal end of the internet in a matter of days. He was a programmer, so at the time, I thought he was doing "work stuff," but after losing too much of my own life to screens, I know better now. There were all those Fridays I'd sit on the front stoop of my mom's townhouse, sometimes for hours, waiting for him to come pick us up for his weekends. At some point, I learned to plan around the truth that six o'clock meant eight o'clock, or maybe nine o'clock in the summer months. I also learned not to ask him for help with anything I assumed to be a quick task unless I had at *least* forty-five minutes to spare.

When I lived with him my junior and senior years of high school, I'd sometimes come home to find the electricity or water had been shut off. I'm pretty sure he made enough money to pay the bills, he just never paid them on time.

I was also always a little offended when Jo and I would ask him a question while he had his face buried in a newspaper or Michael Crichton novel and no fewer than sixty seconds later, he'd pop his head up and say, "Huh? What? Did somebody ask me something?" But now I do it to my family, too.

Where my dad left a trail of Bud Light cans (everywhere), I now leave La Croix cans—usually empty, except for the ones we set down before we're done, then can't remember where we put them or that we put them there at all.

Beyond the walls of our own homes, we've both worked so hard to make it look like we're capable of existing in a world that clearly wasn't built for our brains—with its start times and small talk and real jobs and due-by dates. The truth is, we can only take the same route from Point A to Point B for so long before we feel like we'll die if we have to do it that way one more goddamned time. So instead of falling asleep at the wheel or blowing up our whole lives by leaving yet another city or marriage or job, we meander. We find novelty in the detours and get lost in what we discover, and if it's compelling enough, it's impossible for us to focus on anything else. And sometimes we just plain get lost because we're too busy taking in the new scenery to remember where we turned left.

That's not to say things are easy at home—at least not once we bring unsuspecting partners and children into the mix. Because home is where we unpredictably come alive with the energy to stay up all night if we sense we're *this close* to finding a solution to something or we get inspired to start or finish or start *and* finish a project. Home is where we get mad at you for trying to divert our focus, even if we know we should be doing whatever it is you're reminding us to do (we probably promised you we would, and we believed it, too). It's where we want to fall asleep when we finally allow ourselves to relax for just a minute or two, even if it's when we're supposed to be feeding our kids or getting them ready for school. It's where we're expected to talk to our spouses about bills and the exterminator and what's for dinner even when our brains are overwhelmed from trying so hard to exist out in the neurotypical world that we might very well burst into tears if you press us to decide between grilled chicken and pizza. Home is also where we completely lose our shit (or just shut down completely) when someone criticizes our words or actions because can't you see how hard we're trying to not mess up?! And why don't you understand how exhausting it is?

Compared to my dad, I consider myself lucky that I was "only" in my mid-thirties when I got diagnosed, if for no other reason than it helped explain some of what was going wrong in my marriage before it was too late. It didn't fix anything, but it gave us tools and language to use when looking for solutions. My poor dad has been divorced twice (though for him, the third time really was a charm because my stepmom Pat is the most patient and nonjudgmental person I've ever met). All told, it's my sons who will benefit the most from my diagnosis. If they begin to show signs of neurodivergence, they have parents who will do something. They'll get the kind of compassion and resources my father and I never had.

I could be bitter that no one saw my ADHD—and I should probably be more pissed that when I sensed an issue and went to my mom for help, she didn't do a damn thing—but in the grand scheme of things, I'm not.

Yes, my life is messy. My relationship is messy. My house is messy (the spaces nobody sees, anyway). My finances are incredibly messy. *I am messy*—and I fully admit that a certain amount of privilege has allowed me to stumble through this world and still land where I have. But when I look back on all the missteps and wrong turns I've made, all the times adults failed me when I was a kid, and all the problems I created while taking my own scenic route through life, I mostly come out on the side of being grateful for the journey.

Of course, I occasionally wonder what my life would be like today had I been diagnosed earlier. I hope I'd have more tools for functioning in a relationship, and I imagine I wouldn't owe the IRS $50,000. Maybe I'd have a 401(k)—with money in it! There might be fewer La Croix cans scattered around my house and perhaps I would have aced the GRE and gone on to write the Great American Novel while earning an MFA from a well-respected university.

But if that's the path I'd taken—if I'd somehow managed to find and stay on some sort of main road and ended up more emotionally stable and overall better in the ways society expects me to be—I wouldn't be where I am right now. I probably wouldn't have moved to New York at eighteen with no job or money, and even if I had, there's no way I would have enjoyed the many adventures (and zip codes and hair colors) I did while I was there. I'm guessing I wouldn't have just as impulsively moved back to Kansas City a decade later for a big, cheap apartment with a clawfoot tub and pocket doors, either.

In the *It's a Wonderful Life*-esque montage playing in my head, Well-Adjusted Emily might pay her taxes on time, but she never meets Kyle or gets the chance to be a mom to two sweet boys she loves more than anything in the world. And she definitely doesn't write this book.

The End

Appendix

EmilyFarrisCV-CopyCopyCopyFinal-FINALV2.docx

Emily Farris

LOCATION

Kansas City, MO (But, honestly, I mostly exist on the internet, which means I'm everywhere!)

CONTACT

Yeah, there's no way in hell I'm putting my phone number on a piece of paper that may be printed or forwarded. And I would give you my email address, but there's a very good chance I'll never open your email. And even if I do, the idea of responding in kind will seem exhausting in the moment, so I'll mark it as unread, and then it'll get buried under a million other emails. So just google me and send me a DM on Instagram. I'll engage for a while, then become overwhelmed with the frequency of our correspondence and leave your last message unread for the rest of time.

OBJECTIVE

To fit my entire résumé onto two pages.

EXPERIENCE

- Author | 2021–Present
- Senior Staff Writer, Epicurious | 2021–Present (or at least when I wrote this)
- Podcast Host, *Mother Mother* Podcast | 2021–Present (though on hiatus when I wrote this)
- Freelance Writer, Many Publications You've Actually Heard Of (and Many You Haven't) | 2001–Present
- Freelance Product Photographer | 2019–2021
- Freelance Graphic Designer, Various | 2014–2021
- Freelance Website Designer, Various | 2005–2021
- Freelance Video Editor, Various | 2000–2021
- Recipe Developer, Fancy Small Appliance Brand | 2020–2021
- Virtual Interior Design Consultant, Various | 2020
- Social Media Copywriter, Giant Media Conglomerate I Probably Shouldn't Name | 2020
- Social Media Copywriting Course Creator and Instructor, Self | 2019
- Social Media Consultant and Coach, Various | 2018–2020
- Contract Director of Social Media, Local Coffee Shop Chain | 2018–2019
- Entertaining Columnist, Local Design Magazine | 2018–2019
- Social Media Director, Local Restaurant Group | 2018
- Branded Content Creator, Same Giant Media Conglomerate as Above | 2017–2019
- Event Host and Organizer, Crafting and Cocktail Events for Adults | 2017–2018

- Contributing Production Editor, Major Food Site | 2017
- Contributor/Biweekly Panelist, Local NPR Affiliate | 2015–2018
- Cofounder and Creative Director, Feed Me Creative | 2014–2016
- Cocktail Columnist, MadeMan | 2013–2017
- Vintage Shop "Owner" | 2013
- Cookbook Publicist, Midsize Publishing House | 2013
- Marketing Copywriter, National Medical Nonprofit | 2012
- Communications Manager, Local Coffee Roaster | 2011
- Ghostwriter, Self-Help Relationship Book | 2010–2011
- Daily Deals Copywriter, Not Groupon (but Close) | 2010
- Podcast Host, *Feed Me KC* Podcast | 2009–2011
- Founding Lifestyle Editor, Now-Defunct Kansas City Publication | 2009–2010
- Cocktail Server, Schmancy Hotel Bar | 2009–2010
- Weekend Clerk, Kitchen Supply Store | 2009–2010
- Editor of *Scanner*, Nerve's Pop-Culture Blog | 2008–2010
- Bookstore Clerk, Word Brooklyn | 2008
- Record Store Fill-in Clerk, Okay, I Can't Remember the Name | 2008
- Cookbook Author | 2008
- Lead Tambourinist and Mediocre Backup Singer, Local American Band | 2007–2008
- Volunteer Tutor, Superhero Supply Store | 2007–2008
- Camp Counselor, BEAM Camp | Summer 2007–2008
- Nanny, the Searcy-Stevens Family | 2007
- Freelance Publicist, Various | 2006
- Communications Associate, Environmental Nonprofit | 2005–2006
- Executive Director (Why?), the Federation to Protect the Greenwich Village Waterfront & Great Port | 2005
- Editor in Chief (Again: Why?), Our River, Our Streets (Publication from the Federation) | 2005
- Cofounder and Event Organizer, Bike to Beat Bush | 2004
- Nearly Full-Time Volunteer Director, GOTV Organization | 2004
- Office Administrator, Washington Square United Methodist Church | 2004
- Nanny, the Church Family (No Relation to the Church Where I Worked) | 2003
- Editorial Intern, *Women's Wear Daily* | 2003
- Stringer, the *New York Sun* (Mostly Chuck Schumer and Anthony Weiner Press Conferences) | 2003
- Cocktail Waitress, the Fat Black Pussycat | 2002–2003
- Unlicensed Hair Stylist | 2002–2003
- Editorial Intern, the *New York Sun* | 2002
- Freelance Electrician's Assistant | 2001–2002
- Cocktail Waitress, the Village Underground | 2001–2002
- Stockbroker's Assistant | 2001
- Cocktail Waitress, Barney Mac's | 2000–2001
- Intern, Local Educational Cable Network | 1999–2000
- Intern, Local Country Music Station | 1999–2000
- Tommy Girl Seasonal Fragrance Model, the Jones Store (at the Mall) | Winter 1999
- Hostess, Steak & Ale (Not at the Mall) | 1998–2000
- Cashier, Just For Feet (the World's Largest Athletic Shoe Store! Near the Mall) | 1996–1997
- Cashier, Burger King (Next to the Mall) | 1995
- Cashier, Chinese Delight (in the Food Court at the Mall) | 1994

EDUCATION

- The New School, Bachelor of Liberal Arts | 2002–2006*
- Brooklyn College, Media Studies | 2000–2002

---

*   If proof of degree is required, please contact the school directly. I completed all requirements for graduation but because of administrative issues never collected my degree.

Notes

Epigraph

vii **"My own brain is to me the most unaccountable of machinery":** Lisa Marie Patzer, "Understanding Our Brains Using Interdisciplinary Approaches," SNF Paideia Program at the University of Pennsylvania, March 29, 2021, snfpaideia .upenn.edu/understanding-our-brains-using-interdisciplinary -approaches/.

Introduction

xvi **difficulties with cognitive, organizational, and emotional tasks:** Gil D. Rabinovici, Melanie L. Stephens, and Katherine L. Possin, "Executive Dysfunction," *Behavioral Neurology and Neuropsychiatry* 21, no. 3 (June 2015): 646–659, https://doi .org/10.1212/01.CON.0000466658.05156.54.

xvi **my combined type ADHD:** "Symptoms and Diagnosis of ADHD," Centers for Disease Control and Prevention, last modified August 9, 2022, www.cdc.gov/ncbddd/adhd /diagnosis.html.

xix **"a dysfunction in the brain reward cascade":** Marlene Oscar Berman et al., "Attention-Deficit-Hyperactivity Disorder and Reward Deficiency Syndrome," *Neuropsychiatric Disease and Treatment* 4, no. 5 (November 2008): 893, https://doi.org /10.2147/ndt.s2627.

xx **It's estimated that ten million adults in the United States have ADHD:** Larry Culpepper and Gregory Mattingly, "Challenges in Identifying and Managing Attention-Deficit/ Hyperactivity Disorder in Adults in the Primary Care Setting: A Review of the Literature," *Primary Care Companion to the Journal of Clinical Psychiatry* 12, no. 6 (2010): e1–e7, https: //doi.org/10.4088/pcc.10r00951pur.

xxi **a neurodevelopmental "disorder" that's usually diagnosed in childhood:** "What Is ADHD?" Centers for Disease Control and Prevention, last modified August 9, 2022, www.cdc.gov /ncbddd/adhd/facts.html.

xxi **a dysfunction in the dopaminergic system:** Edna Grünblatt, Anna Maria Werling, Alexander Roth, Marcel Romanos, and Susanne Walitza, "Association Study and a Systematic Meta-Analysis of the VNTR Polymorphism in the 3'-UTR of Dopamine Transporter Gene and Attention-Deficit Hyperactivity Disorder," *Journal of Neural Transmission* 126, no. 4 (March 28, 2019): 517–529, https://doi.org/10.1007 /s00702-019-01998-x.

xxi **Dopamine controls numerous brain functions:** Shannon Johnson, "What Is the Link Between ADHD and Dopamine?" Medical News Today, June 18, 2019, www.medicalnewstoday .com/articles/325499.

xxi–xxii **the first textbook description of a condition that presented as ADHD:** Russell A. Barkley and Helmut Peters, "The Earliest Reference to ADHD in the Medical Literature? Melchior Adam Weikard's Description in 1775 of 'Attention Deficit' (Mangel Der Aufmerksamkeit, Attentio Volubilis)," *Journal of Attention Disorders* 16, no. 8 (February 8, 2012): 623–630, https://doi.org/10.1177/1087054711432309.

xxii **first recorded description of ADHD was published in 1902:** Klaus W. Lange, Susanne Reichl, Katharina M. Lange,

Lara Tucha, and Oliver Tucha, "The History of Attention Deficit Hyperactivity Disorder," *ADHD Attention Deficit and Hyperactivity Disorders* 2, no. 4 (November 30, 2010): 241–255, https://doi.org/10.1007/s12402-010-0045-8.

xxii **Neurodiverse versus Neurodivergent:** Nicole Baumer and Julia Frueh, "What Is Neurodiversity?" *Harvard Health*, November 23, 2021, www.health.harvard.edu/blog/what-is-neurodiversity-202111232645.

xxiii **Executive Dysfunction:** Gil D. Rabinovici, Melanie L. Stephens, and Katherine L. Possin, "Executive Dysfunction," *Behavioral Neurology and Neuropsychiatry* 21, no. 3 (June 2015): 646–659, https://doi.org/10.1212/01.CON .0000466658.05156.54.

xxiii **Hyperfixation:** Amanda Barrell, "ADHD and Hyperfocus: What Is It, and How Can I Manage It?" Medical News Today, July 8, 2019, www.medicalnewstoday.com/articles/325681.

xxiii **Time Blindness:** M. J. Dengsø, "Wrong Brains at the Wrong Time? Understanding ADHD Through the Diachronic Constitution of Minds," *Advances in Neurodevelopmental Disorders* 6 (2022): 184–195, https://doi.org/10.1007 /s41252-022-00244-y.

xxiv **Emotional Regulation:** Elizabeth A. Steinberg and Deborah A. G. Drabick, "A Developmental Psychopathology Perspective on ADHD and Comorbid Conditions: The Role of Emotion Regulation," *Child Psychiatry & Human Development* 46, no. 6 (February 7, 2015): 951–966, https://doi.org/10.1007/s10578 -015-0534-2.

xxiv **not formally recognized as a disorder:** "Rejection Sensitive Dysphoria (RSD): Symptoms & Treatment," Cleveland Clinic, last reviewed August 30, 2022, my.clevelandclinic.org/health /diseases/24099-rejection-sensitive-dysphoria-rsd.

xxiv **Sensory Processing Issues:** Ahmad Ghanizadeh, "Sensory Processing Problems in Children with ADHD, a Systematic Review," *Psychiatry Investigation* 8, no. 2 (2011): 89, https://doi.org/10.4306/pi.2011.8.2.89.

How We Got Here

6   **"ADHD Is Different for Women":** Maria Yagoda, "ADHD Is Different for Women," *The Atlantic*, April 3, 2013, www.theatlantic.com/health/archive/2013/04/adhd-is-different-for-women/381158/.

7   **I'd done enough of my own research:** Patricia O. Quinn and Manisha Madhoo, "A Review of Attention-Deficit/Hyperactivity Disorder in Women and Girls," *Primary Care Companion for CNS Disorders* 16, no. 3 (May 15, 2014), https://doi.org/10.4088/pcc.13r01596.

8   **many of my flaws were likely ADHD symptoms:** "Symptoms and Diagnosis of ADHD," Centers for Disease Control and Prevention, last modified August 9, 2022, www.cdc.gov/ncbddd/adhd/diagnosis.html.

Everything, All the Time

18   ***Don't Sweat the Small Stuff:*** Richard Carlson, *Don't Sweat the Small Stuff—and It's All Small Stuff: Simple Ways to Keep the Little Things from Taking over Your Life* (New York: Hyperion, 1997).

20   **how ADHD affects women and girls:** Patricia O. Quinn and Manisha Madhoo, "A Review of Attention-Deficit/Hyperactivity Disorder in Women and Girls," *Primary Care Companion for CNS Disorders* 16, no. 3 (May 15, 2014), https://doi.org/10.4088/pcc.13r01596.

Seventeen Little Stories

34   *Drinking: A Love Story*: Caroline Knapp, *Drinking: A Love Story* (New York: Dial Press, 2005).

Lipstick Is the Only Makeup You Can Put On in Public

54   **Garner Ted Armstrong:** Douglas Martin, "Garner Ted Armstrong, Evangelist, 73, Dies," *New York Times*, September 17, 2003, www.nytimes.com/2003/09/17/us/garner-ted -armstrong-evangelist-73-dies.html.

Street Drugs

64   **the literal Methamphetamine Capital of America:** David Martin, "Independence's Rap as Meth City USA Needs Tweaking," *The Pitch*, October 19, 2011, www.thepitchkc.com /independences-rap-as-meth-city-usa-needs-tweaking/.

64   **by *Rolling Stone* magazine in the nineties:** Peter Wilkinson, "America's Drug: Postcards from Tweakville," *Rolling Stone*, February 19, 1998.

66   **Desoxyn:** "Desoxyn—FDA Prescribing Information, Side Effects and Uses," Drugs.com, www.drugs.com/pro/desoxyn .html.

66   **methamphetamine predates the FDA by thirteen years:** Shaobin Yu, Ling Zhu, Qiang Shen, Xue Bai, and Xuhui Di, "Recent Advances in Methamphetamine Neurotoxicity Mechanisms and Its Molecular Pathophysiology," *Behavioural Neurology* 2015 (2015), https://doi.org/10.1155/2015/103969; "FDA History," FDA, June 29, 2018, www.fda.gov/about-fda /fda-history.

67   *The Class of 2000: A Definitive Study of the New Generation*: CBS News, *The Class of 2000* (New York: Simon & Schuster, 2000).

67   **equated a brain on drugs with a fried egg:** Partnership for a Drug-Free America, "This Is Your Brain, This Is Drugs, This Is Your Brain on Drugs" [poster], Images from the History of Medicine (IHM) collection, collections.nlm.nih.gov/catalog /nlm:nlmuid-101437932-img.

71   **phentermine—an M.D.-prescribed "amphetamine substitute":** "Substituted Amphetamine," Wikipedia, last modified March 16, 2023, en.wikipedia.org/wiki/Substituted _amphetamine.

75   **people with ADHD are prone to drug and alcohol abuse:** Courtney A. Zulauf, Susan E. Sprich, Steven A. Safren, and Timothy E. Wilens, "The Complicated Relationship Between Attention Deficit/Hyperactivity Disorder and Substance Use Disorders," *Current Psychiatry Reports* 16, no. 3 (February 15, 2014), https://doi.org/10.1007/s11920-013-0436-6.

75   **Vyvanse is such a controlled substance:** Vyvanse™ (lisdexamfetamine dimesylate) Medication Guide, https: //www.accessdata.fda.gov/drugsatfda_docs/label/2007 /021977lbl.pdf.

75   **all those trolls and quacks who claim "ADHD isn't real":** Deborah Carpenter, "How to Silence ADHD Naysayers," *ADDitude*, October 6, 2006, www.additudemag.com/silence -naysayers-adhd-myths-facts/.

Self-Assessment

91   **Self-Assessment: Adult ADHD Self-Report Scale v1.1:** R. C. Kessler et al., "The World Health Organization Adult ADHD Self-Report Scale (ASRS)," *Psychological Medicine* 35, no. 2 (2005): 245–256. https://www.hcp.med.harvard.edu/ncs/asrs.php.

93 **Dropbox is a total racket:** Ady88, "Shared Folders, Why Do I Have to Pay for Someone Else's Files?" Dropboxforum.com, February 26, 2020, www.dropboxforum.com/t5/Create-upload -and-share/Shared-folders-why-do-I-have-to-pay-for-someone -elses-files/td-p/399233.

No, I Will Not Shut Up About My Abortion

105 **known then as the Margaret Sanger Clinic:** Karen Matthews, "Sanger's Name to Be Dropped from NYC Clinic over Eugenics," AP News, April 22, 2021, apnews.com/article/us -news-health-new-york-manhattan-race-and-ethnicity -ddef4d3812cfe106b7c0844536ac37ec.

107 **which did happen the following year:** Julie Rovner, "Timeline: The Debate over Plan B," NPR, August 28, 2006, www.npr.org/2006/08/28/5725514/timeline-the-debate-over -plan-b.

Ten Things I Hate About Fruit

110 **Apple seeds have cyanide in them:** Melissa Petruzzello, "Can Apple Seeds Kill You?" *Encyclopaedia Britannica*, 2019, www .britannica.com/story/can-apple-seeds-kill-you.

110 **underripe lychee can cause a blood pressure crash:** Meera Senthilingam, "Natural-Born Killers: The Fruits and Veggies That Could Poison You," CNN, April 10, 2017, www.cnn.com /2017/04/10/health/fruits-poison-litchee-ackee-nerve-disease /index.html.

110–111 **medium-size banana has 27 grams of carbs:** "FoodData Central," USDA, April 1, 2019, fdc.nal.usda.gov/fdc-app .html#/food-details/173944/nutrients.

111 **that's nine *more* grams than a beef soft taco from Taco Bell:** "Taco Bell Nutrition Information," Taco Bell, www.tacobell .com/nutrition/info.

Misdiagnosed

113 **"Hysteria is undoubtedly"**: Cecilia Tasca, Mariangela Rapetti, Mauro Giovanni Carta, and Bianca Fadda, "Women and Hysteria in the History of Mental Health," *Clinical Practice & Epidemiology in Mental Health* 8, no. 1 (October 19, 2012): 110–119, https://doi.org/10.2174/1745017901208010110.

114 **"Difficulties in social interactions in girls"**: Patricia O. Quinn and Manisha Madhoo, "A Review of Attention-Deficit/ Hyperactivity Disorder in Women and Girls," *Primary Care Companion for CNS Disorders* 16, no. 3 (May 15, 2014), https://doi.org/10.4088/pcc.13r01596.

116 **"Missed diagnosis of ADHD in women and girls"**: Patricia O. Quinn and Manisha Madhoo, "A Review of Attention-Deficit/ Hyperactivity Disorder in Women and Girls," *Primary Care Companion for CNS Disorders* 16, no. 3 (May 15, 2014), https://doi.org/10.4088/pcc.13r01596.

118 **"It is important to move away"**: Susan Young et al., "Females with ADHD: An Expert Consensus Statement Taking a Lifespan Approach Providing Guidance for the Identification and Treatment of Attention-Deficit/Hyperactivity Disorder in Girls and Women," *BMC Psychiatry* 20, no. 1 (2020): 1–27, https://doi.org/10.1186/s12888-020-02707-9.

119 **"Female patients primarily exhibiting symptoms"**: Patricia O. Quinn and Manisha Madhoo, "A Review of Attention-Deficit/ Hyperactivity Disorder in Women and Girls," *Primary Care Companion for CNS Disorders* 16, no. 3 (May 15, 2014), https://doi.org/10.4088/pcc.13r01596.

121 **"Greater awareness on the part of healthcare professionals"**: Patricia O. Quinn and Manisha Madhoo, "A Review of Attention-Deficit/Hyperactivity Disorder in Women and Girls," *Primary Care Companion for CNS Disorders* 16, no. 3 (May 15, 2014), https://doi.org/10.4088/pcc.13r01596.

A Tale of Two Summers

147 **apparently never-ending pandemic:** World Health Organization, "Coronavirus Disease (COVID-19) Pandemic," World Health Organization, 2022, www.who.int/europe /emergencies/situations/covid-19.

147 **the era of that orange piece of shit:** Michael Dimock and John Gramlich, "How America Changed During Trump's Presidency," Pew Research Center, January 29, 2021, www .pewresearch.org/2021/01/29/how-america-changed-during -donald-trumps-presidency/.

147 **Bad men were finally being called out for their bad behavior:** Alix Langone, "#MeToo and Time's Up Founders Explain the Difference Between the 2 Movements—and How They're Alike," *Time*, March 8, 2018, time.com/5189945 /whats-the-difference-between-the-metoo-and-times-up -movements/.

147 **one of them was about to be nominated for the Supreme Court:** Sheryl Gay Stolberg, "Kavanaugh Is Sworn In After Close Confirmation Vote in Senate," *New York Times*, October 6, 2018, www.nytimes.com/2018/10/06/us/politics/brett -kavanaugh-supreme-court.html.

149 **a shot of her own thrifted owl basket:** @Simplychi, Instagram post, May 30, 2018, www.instagram.com/p/BjbBC8Gg8mp/.

150 **It was *the* owl basket:** @thatemilyfarris, Instagram post, July 16, 2018, www.instagram.com/p/BlTV79cnYyr/.

The ADHD Taxman Cometh

161 **"ADHD tax":** Rick Webster, "The ADHD Tax Is Draining— Financially and Emotionally," *ADDitude*, October 17, 2022, www.additudemag.com/adhd-tax-financial-wellness-money -problems/.

166 **$35 overdraft fees:** Kori Hale, "Bank of America Easing Up on Hated Overdraft Fees," *Forbes*, January 23, 2022, www .forbes.com/sites/korihale/2022/01/23/bank-of-america -easing-up-on-hated-overdraft-fees/.

You Don't Want to Be in Love, You Want to Be in Love in a Movie

177 **You Don't Want to Be in Love, You Want to Be in Love in a Movie:** Quotes from *Sleepless in Seattle*, IMDb, www.imdb .com/title/tt0108160/quotes/qt0293327.

178 **sixteen million subscribers paying for AOL at the time:** Leslie Walker, "Rivals Cede Throne to AOL," *Washington Post*, April 8, 1999, www.washingtonpost.com/archive/business /1999/04/08/rivals-cede-throne-to-aol/6782e694-4f8c-4a42 -8314-8adde5d5777c/.

178 **Love@AOL:** Susan Carpenter, "Screening Mates at Love@ AOL," *Los Angeles Times*, December 24, 1998, www.latimes .com/archives/la-xpm-1998-dec-24-cl-57025-story.html.

182 ***Sleepless in Seattle*:** Nora Ephron, director, *Sleepless in Seattle* (TriStar Pictures, 1993).

184 ***Groundhog Day*:** Harold Ramis, director, *Groundhog Day* (Columbia Pictures, 1993).

Things I've Forgotten and Things I Don't Think I'll Ever Forget

196 **the official theme song of the DARE program:** Teresa Jennings, "My Mind Is Mine," Music K-8, May 1992, www .musick8.com/html/current_tune.php?numbering =10&songorder=1.

197 **in his 2006 novel *Absurdistan*:** Gary Shteyngart, *Absurdistan* (New York: Random House, 2005).

Me, Myself, and My Never-Ending Postpartum Anxiety

200 **for safe sleep:** "Safe Sleep for Babies," Centers for Disease Control and Prevention, November 27, 2018, www.cdc.gov /vitalsigns/safesleep/index.html.

205 **what was happening in China and Italy:** AJMC Staff, "A Timeline of COVID-19 Developments in 2020," *American Journal of Managed Care*, last modified January 1, 2021, www .ajmc.com/view/a-timeline-of-covid19-developments-in-2020.

205 **disinfected the groceries:** Maria Godoy, "No, You Don't Need to Disinfect Your Groceries. But Here's How to Shop Safely," NPR, April 12, 2020, www.npr.org/sections/health-shots /2020/04/12/832269202/no-you-dont-need-to-disinfect-your -groceries-but-here-s-to-shop-safely.

206 **ADHD superpower:** Jane Ann Sedgwick, Andrew Merwood, and Philip Asherson, "The Positive Aspects of Attention Deficit Hyperactivity Disorder: A Qualitative Investigation of Successful Adults with ADHD," *ADHD Attention Deficit and Hyperactivity Disorders* 11, no. 11 (October 29, 2018): 241–253, https://doi.org/10.1007/s12402-018-0277-6.

210 **recent studies have put the heritability around 80 percent:** Oliver Grimm, Thorsten M. Kranz, and Andreas Reif, "Genetics of ADHD: What Should the Clinician Know?" *Current Psychiatry Reports* 22, no. 18 (February 27, 2020), https://doi.org/10.1007/s11920-020-1141-x.

A Shed of One's Own

211 **In *A Room of One's Own*, Virginia Woolf famously declared:** Virginia Woolf, *A Room of One's Own* (London: Hogarth Press, 1929).

Color of the Year

218 **"Perceptually and cognitively, men and women":** Nidhi
     Jaint et al., "Gender Based Alteration in Color Perception,"
     Indian Journal of Physiology and Pharmacology 54, no.
     4 (October 1, 2010): 366–370, pubmed.ncbi.nlm.nih
     .gov/21675035/.

219 **A color-blind person doesn't see the world in grayscale:**
     National Eye Institute, "Color Blindness," National Eye
     Institute, National Institutes of Health, July 3, 2019, www.nei
     .nih.gov/learn-about-eye-health/eye-conditions-and-diseases
     /color-blindness.

219 **it's that I focus *too* much once something has commanded
     my attention:** Rony Sklar, "Hyperfocus in Adult ADHD: An
     EEG Study of the Differences in Cortical Activity in Resting
     and Arousal States" (master's thesis), 2013, https://www
     .researchgate.net/publication/259681620.

220 **Pantone's Color of the Year is called Very Peri:** "Pantone
     Color of the Year 2022: Introduction," Pantone, 2022, www
     .pantone.com/color-of-the-year-2022.

Yes, I Have a Body

221 **that June 1993 *Seventeen* magazine cover:** Anne Helen
     Petersen, "The Millennial Vernacular of Fatphobia," *Culture
     Study*, May 23, 2021, annehelen.substack.com/p/the
     -millennial-vernacular-of-fatphobia.

The Scenic Route

237 **a reference to a *Seinfeld* episode titled "The Opposite":**
     Andy Cowan, Larry David, and Jerry Seinfeld, "The Opposite"
     (episode aired May 19, 1994), *Seinfeld*, IMDb, www.imdb
     .com/title/tt0697744/.

239 **nearly half of all parents with ADHD go on to have
     neurodivergent kids:** K. Blum et al., "Attention-Deficit-
     Hyperactivity Disorder and Reward Deficiency Syndrome,"
     Neuropsychiatric Disease and Treatment 4, no. 5 (November
     2008): 893, https://doi.org/10.2147/ndt.s2627.

Acknowledgments

B ecause I have so many people to thank that I don't want to waste words on flowery transitions—and also because my brain does better with bullet points than a big block of prose—here's a likely incomplete list of the folks who made this book possible.

- My editor, Alison Dalafave, who enthusiastically acquired my first memoir and patiently guided me through the hardest part (writing it) in all the ways my brain needed.
- Gwen Hawkes, who fearlessly took the reins from Alison and didn't make me cut all of my em dashes and asides at the last minute.
- My agent, Michael Bourret, who signed me before either of us had wrinkles. I was big on ideas and short on focus back then, and I'm so grateful you stuck with me all this time.
- Gina Kaufmann, who helped me find the real story in a far less exciting version—and who was always willing to look at early drafts. Your feedback and friendship are gifts I do not take for granted.

264

Acknowledgments

- Sarah Herrington, for rescuing me from the agony of perfection paralysis more times than I can count.
- Emily Flake, Lyz Lenz, and Amy Shearn, for reading essays I wasn't sure were even essays. And for helping me see that they were worthy of ending up in print.
- Luke Wetzel, who championed this book from the start.
- Meredith Hoffa, who first gave me a platform on What's Up Moms to write about my ADHD diagnosis and my mental health after having kids.
- Michelle Woo, for letting me write about my postpartum anxiety (and adorable baby farts!) for a Lifehacker piece that I adapted into a longer essay in this book.
- Kristy Firebaugh, who could probably make a career out of beta reading.
- Irina Gonzales and Elizabeth Brink, for your invaluable and insightful feedback.
- The instructors and fellow participants in my many writing workshops (Catapult, Grub Street, Sackett Street, CNF, and Writing Co-Lab), who continuously inspired me to put words on the page when I was sure I didn't have anything left to say. I don't think any of you understand quite how much I needed your encouragement and support.
- Kelly Glass, I've learned more from you than you even know.

- Robert Bair, for giving me your blessing to write my truth. And for always championing my voice.
- Emily Johnson, for being flexible when I needed it most. And for reminding me that I'm allowed to rest.
- Maria Yagoda: You don't know me, but your article in *The Atlantic* changed my life.
- Dr. B and Dr. U, for truly listening to me.
- Ruth and Fred Hopkins, for the village you've built around us. And for helping with the laundry when I just couldn't.
- And last, but certainly not least, Kyle, who did lots of overtime with our beautiful boys so that I could carve out the time and space to write this book. Thank you for continuing to love me (and feed me) even when I was at my burnt-out, sleep-deprived worst.

About the Author

Emily Farris is a writer who dabbles in design and sporadically hosts the *Mother Mother* podcast. In fifth grade, she won the DARE essay contest. Since then, she's written for *The Cut, Bon Appetit, Epicurious, Architectural Digest, ELLE Decor, BuzzFeed, Lifehacker, Cool Hunting, What's Up Moms, Food52, The Daily Beast*, and other outlets you've actually heard of. Emily lives in Kansas City, Missouri, with her husband, sons, and a few animals.

Facebook: www.facebook.com/thatemilyfarris
Instagram: @thatemilyfarris
Website: www.thatemilyfarris.com